MASS UNEMPLOYMENT
Plant Closings and Community Mental Health

by
TERRY F. BUSS and F. STEVENS REDBURN
with JOSEPH WALDRON

Volume 6, Sage Studies in Community Mental Health

SAGE PUBLICATIONS
Beverly Hills / London / New Delhi

Cover photography by Paul B. Shell, reprinted with permission of the
Youngstown Vindicator.

For information address:

SAGE Publications, Inc.
275 South Beverly Drive
Beverly Hills, California 90212

SAGE Publications India Pvt. Ltd.
C-236 Defence Colony
New Delhi 110 024, India

SAGE Publications Ltd
28 Banner Street
London EC1Y 8QE, England

Printed in the United States of America

Library of Congress Cataloging in Publication Data

Buss, Terry F.
    Mass Unemployment.

    (Sage studies in community mental health : v. 6)
    Bibliography: P.
    1. Unemployment—United States—Psychological aspects.
2. Plant shutdowns—United States—Psychological aspects.
3. Community mental health services—United States.
I. Redburn, F. Stevens. II. Waldron, Joseph.
III. Title. IV. Series.
HD5708.B87   1983   331.13'73'0973   83-4450

ISBN 0-8039-2012-1
ISBN 0-8039-2013-X (pbk.)

FIRST PRINTING

MASS UNEMPLOYMENT

Sage Studies in Community Mental Health 6

SAGE STUDIES IN COMMUNITY MENTAL HEALTH

Series Editor: **Richard H. Price**
Community Psychology Program,
University of Michigan

SAGE STUDIES IN COMMUNITY MENTAL HEALTH is a book series consisting of both single-authored and co-authored monographs and concisely edited collections of original articles which deal with issues and themes of current concern in the community mental health and related fields. Drawing from research in a variety of disciplines, the series seeks to link the work of the scholar and practitioner in this field, as well as advance the state of current knowledge in community mental health.

Volumes in this series:

1. Gary VandenBos (Editor): *PSYCHOTHERAPY: Practice, Research, Policy*
2. Cary Cherniss: *STAFF BURNOUT: Job Stress in the Human Services*
3. Richard F. Ketterer: *CONSULTATION AND EDUCATION IN MENTAL HEALTH: Problems and Prospects*
4. Benjamin H. Gottlieb (Editor): *SOCIAL NETWORKS AND SOCIAL SUPPORT*
5. Morton O. Wagenfeld, Paul V. Lemkau, and Blair Justice (Editors): *PUBLIC MENTAL HEALTH: Perspectives and Prospects*
6. Terry F. Buss, F. Stevens Redburn, with Joseph Waldron, *MASS UNEMPLOYMENT: Plant Closings and Community Mental Health*

Additional Volumes in Preparation

For the Steelworkers and Their Families

Contents

List of Tables and Figures

Acknowledgments

The research reported here would not have been possible without the individual contributions of dozens of people. We are particularly indebted to Dee Roth, Chief of Program Evaluation and Research of the Ohio Department of Mental Health and to Elliott Liebow and Hal Vreeland of the Center for Work and Mental Health of the National Institute of Mental Health. Both organizations provided the necessary funding for the project. Equally important was the cooperation, support, and encouragement we received throughout the project.

A project of this scope and magnitude required a major commitment of time and energy from a variety of researchers in our organization. Carla Wilson and Mindy Kimmelman, who each served as managers on the project, expertly coordinated the activities of staff workers in the field and conducted much of the data analysis. George Cheney, a coauthor of Chapter 5, worked hard on much of the case study and secondary data analysis.

The project received a great deal of research and technical support from various departments at Youngstown State University. Hildegard Schnuttgen, Louise Karns, and Debbie Beronja, of our library's Reference Department, were extremely important in locating or acquiring reference materials used in the study. Mary Ann Murray, Tom Kiger, and Carl Leet of our Media Center bailed us out on several occasions with the rapid production of professional graphs and diagrams. Fred Ullam, Tom Davidson, and Rich Rolland of our Computer Center kept our project afloat by developing complex computer programs that greatly simplified the analysis of our extensive data files. Judith Ferrett deserves special thanks for the rapid and efficient typing of our manuscript in its multiple drafts. Carla Wilson expertly proofread the manuscript as it was continually revised.

Many other people, too numerous to mention here, deserve our thanks for helping to bring the various parts of this project together. We deeply appreciate their efforts on our behalf.

Series Editor's Preface

Recent changes in our economic circumstances, particularly in the industrial states, have made us increasingly aware of the personal and psychological impact of mass unemployment. The distress of displaced workers and their families is now no longer only portrayed in scientific reports but is documented in the mass media and debated in the halls of Congress.

But community mental health workers have not found it easy to respond to this source of psychological distress in so many of our communities. Part of the responsibility lies with a community mental health system whose orientation in the recent past has been largely due to severe and chronic mental health problems rather than to the normal crises of everyday life. In addition, workers don't wish to see themselves as in need of psychological help and do not necessarily see mental health services as relevant to their problem. But the fact is that many unemployed workers and their families are experiencing significant psychological distress and the toll of mass unemployment is real. How can the community mental health movement respond?

In this thoughtful book, Buss, Redburn, and Waldron examine the psychological, social and economic impact of mass unemployment, the issues raised by unemployment, and the service and policy alternatives available to the community in general, and the community mental health professionals in particular. The authors begin by reviewing the scientific literature on the impact of unemployment. They then review their own research in Youngstown, Ohio, a steel mill town hard hit by the recent recession and declining demand for steel. They examine both the psychological impact and the community response to unemployment using both survey methods and case studies that illuminate the circumstances of laid off workers. Their data provide a rich and revealing portrait of a community and its workers coping with the shock of unemployment.

This research team goes further, however, and documents the community mental health responses to mass unemployment in Youngstown. They describe the services that emerged and the community's response to those services. They find that most workers perceive traditional mental health services as irrelevant to their problems, or are unaware of the more appropriate services that have been made available. Frequently, workers who have used the services felt discouraged from further help seeking.

Buss and his colleagues then propose a thoughtful plan for mental health service responses that can help to assess and meet the needs of displaced workers. They describe policies that, if enacted by communities, employers, and legislators, could substantially reduce the impact of unemployment on communities and individual workers.

Employment transitions will continue to be a major source of distress and a major challenge to human and social adaptation through the rest of this decade and perhaps even further into the future. Buss and his colleagues have provided us with a provocative summary of the scientific information and policy alternatives to help the community mental health and other human service workers to both understand and respond to the needs of displaced workers in our communities.

—*Richard H. Price*

Chapter 1

JOB LOSS AND
MENTAL HEALTH

In the 1930s, a great world depression produced the first systematic, sociological studies of job loss and unemployment and their effects on individuals, families, and communities. In the intervening forty years, the problem of unemployment seemed to merge with that of poverty, its causes, and its effects. By the 1960s, when the U.S. community mental health movement was defining and launching its programs, attention was focused on those left behind by economic growth—"the poor"— including many victims of past and present racial discrimination. Only in the last half decade or so has the faltering of the U.S. and European economies produced a significant new wave of public and scholarly interest in job loss and unemployment as job problems distinct from those of chronic poverty.

JOB LOSS AND STRESS

Business and farm bankruptcies, layoffs in heavy manufacturing industries, the permanent closing of obsolete plants and marginal mining operations, and other similar events have altered the lives of millions of workers and their families. As of mid-1982, nearly ten percent of the U.S. labor force (including only those actively seeking work) was, at least for the moment, unemployed. Perhaps more disturbing, three times that number would be told some time during the year that they were out of a job. Of the major external shocks that can alter a person's life, only the death of a loved one, a major illness, or divorce affect as many.

Economic changes reshaping the advanced industrial nations in the early 1980s call our attention to job loss and unemployment as sources of stress. As in the Depression of the 1930s, prolonged unemployment has become a common experience among people with histories of stable employment. These are often highly skilled individuals, whose loss of work and failure to find new jobs tells them that their skills are no longer needed or valued. Also, as in the Depression era, the proportion of people out of work in some states and communities and the average duration of unemployment have been such as to strain the abilities of governments to provide alternative income or benefits, of communities to offer less formal kinds of economic and social support, and of families to sustain themselves.

Because most people both need and like their jobs, there is no question that involuntary layoff or termination is stressful for most people. It is not obvious, however, whether job losses and unemployment should be a focus of mental health policy and programs. That it should be depends on the answers to many questions to be enumerated in the following sections of this chapter and explored in the chapters that follow. But, first, it is useful to examine the beliefs that helped launch and that underpin the original community mental health movement, especially the belief in strategies of prevention.

PREVENTION AND THE COMMUNITY
MENTAL HEALTH MOVEMENT

In 1963, when President Kennedy proposed the Community Mental Health Centers Act, he spoke of the need for "specific programs directed . . . at known causes, and the strengthening of our fundamental community, social welfare, and vocational programs which can do much to eliminate or correct the harsh environmental conditions which often are associated with mental retardation and mental illness" (Kennedy, 1963). However, this statement does not reflect the reality of the program's early years. Initially, prevention activities were given neither the political clout nor the monetary resources to fulfill their mission. Nor have recent changes in the mental health centers program encouraged in any way the commitment of substantial resources to such proactive programs. Nevertheless, the belief in prevention as a goal survives; the past twenty years have provided enough practical experience to support some optimism about its future.

Richard Price and his associates (1980, p. 20) have concluded that "progress toward the goal of prevention has been substantial." The President's Commission on Mental Health in 1978 endorsed "a concerted national effort to prevent mental disabilities" (1978). However, as Catalano and Dooley (1979) note, the Commission's Research Task Panel was more cautious than its Prevention Task Panel, suggesting that much research was needed before practical programs to prevent mental disorders could be undertaken.

In any case, the first two decades of community mental health provide very few examples of programs for individuals or groups designed to meet the particular mental health needs of people thrown out of work. The movement emerged during an era when majority affluence was assumed. Unemployment was generally transient and short-term, being associated with business cycles; government fiscal policies seemed capable of controlling these cycles and an increasing array of public employment benefits, training, and public employment programs were available to soften the effects of job loss.

Only a supposedly diminishing residual group—the poor—were not at least partially insulated from economic hardship. For the poor, many of them victims of racial discrimination or other institutional causes of a lack of early opportunity, frequent or chronic unemployment was (and is) part of a syndrome that locked them out of a share of affluence. Thus the early focus of the community mental health movement, and in fact a major component of the ideology that drove and justified the movement, was poverty and the associated denial of economic opportunity.

Because the community mental health centers were established during such a period, their clinical and outreach orientations did not anticipate mental health needs associated with massive job losses among experienced workers. Insofar as a center emphasized prevention activities (and many did not), it was likely to concentrate attention on the poor or on noneconomic stressors: divorced and separated persons, victims of violence, drug and alcohol abusers. As a result, only a handful of centers have the experience and the capacity for dealing with massive job losses among workers whose previous experience did not prepare them for this sudden threat to their future economic status and security.

The issues of whether or how to serve this group have emerged, not surprisingly, at a time of fiscal constraint. This reduces the opportunity for experimentation and innovation. The present is also inopportune because the growing reliance on fees for service and third-party payments as sources of program income provides no financing mechanism for prevention programs aimed at the newly unemployed. Finally, support for prevention programs is still tenuous and uneven. This is due not only to the continued strength of a "biomedical model" that emphasizes the internal rather than the external causes of mental disorder. The lack of support for prevention programs is also due to the strength of other service demands and legal mandates on the time and resources of the centers, especially the mandate to serve ever-growing numbers of deinstitutionalized former mental hospital patients.

Now, when major job losses have occurred in hundreds of communities, their mental health centers and other human service agencies find themselves in a bind. They have little in their previous programmatic experience on which to draw. The few previous prevention efforts in other communities have not been well publicized or independently evaluated; and, funds or financing mechanisms to support special programs for the unemployed are usually absent. These are the realities that must be addressed by anyone interested in reducing the damage to these communities that may stem from massive and prolonged unemployment.

A SPECIFICATION OF THE PROBLEM

The problem is to construct effective programs of primary prevention aimed at groups at risk of mental disorders due to job loss and unemployment. As with the development of other prevention programs, addressing this problem means following a long and difficult intellectual path. A series of research questions must be posed and answered systematically before there is a sound basis for action. These questions are presented below:

(A) *How frequently and under what circumstances are the stresses produced by loss of work sufficient to bring on emotional disorder?*

(B) *What do the established associations between national unemployment rates and higher aggregate levels of suicide, mental hospital admission, and other stress measures indicate about the effects of job losses?*

It is fairly certain that job loss and unemployment produce dangerous increases in personal stress. For instance, the work of Harvey Brenner (1973, 1976) provides convincing evidence that higher aggregate levels of unemployment have, over the years, been associated with higher levels of social disorder, including mental hospital first admissions and the suicide rate. However, such associations immediately raise other questions. Who is most vulnerable to such stress and why? Are experienced, high-wage, unionized workers subject to the same pressures as others? Or are they able to pass the burden of unemployment, and its associated pressures, onto other less competitive job seekers? Are massive job losses as likely to produce stress as individual firings? Do short-term layoffs associated with the business cycle have different effects than permanent losses due to plant closings, bankruptcies, and similar events?

Among a group of terminated employees, which are the most likely to experience severe emotional distress? Does job loss actually produce mental illness in some people; or is it merely the triggering agent that "uncovers" preexisting mental disorders (Catalano & Dooley, 1979)? How important are such social factors as support from family and friends in conditioning the psychological impact of job loss?

Perhaps even more important, what in the dynamics of the job loss experience itself produces the stress? Is it the immediate shock of the event that does damage or the cumulative impacts of many days or months without work? How important is the loss of valued status in producing psychological distress? How important is the loss of income and gradual accumulation of economic hardships and pressures?

(C) *What are the sequence and timing of individual reactions to job loss and unemployment?*

Closely related to questions of dynamics are questions concerning the timing or staging of stresses and their psychological effects. Are damaging levels of anxiety produced during the prelayoff period by an atmosphere of rumor and uncertainty? How often does the first shock of job loss cause people to react violently or to fall into severe depression? Do the effects of job loss typically decay or build in the weeks after the event? Do most individuals go through predictable stages of reaction—shock, denial, grief, recovery—or does the order and timing of reactions greatly vary from one person to another?

The answers to questions about timing and sequence of effects have strong implications for the design of prevention programs. If most effects occur early and are concentrated in a brief interval, then mass prelayoff interventions assume great importance. If the effects accumulate slowly, then there will be more benefit in efforts to identify people at special risk and more time to design interventions targeted at subgroups of the unemployed. Finally, if the timing of impacts varies from person to person, this perhaps suggests a need to monitor individuals over time and to tailor interventions to fit a variety of personal needs.

(D) *Which people are most vulnerable to the stresses produced by job loss and are, therefore, at special risk of mental or emotional disorder?*

Within any group of terminated workers, the meaning and impact of the experience will vary depending on each person's current situation, personal history, access to material resources, social support, coping skills, and so on. These are, in turn, a function partly of such readily measured attributes as age, education, previous job status, and race/ethnicity. How important are these attributes in explaining emotional reactions to job loss? Can they be used to predict which subgroups of terminated employees are at special risk of developing severe emotional disorders? In particular, does past or present racial discrimination place minority workers at a special disadvantage in coping with job loss and avoiding severe stress reactions?

(E) *Aside from its effects on the incidence of emotional disorders, are there other ways in which job loss constitutes a mental health problem?*

Mental health may be defined, negatively and narrowly, as the absence of emotional disorder; or it may be defined positively as the presence of certain capacities or states of mind. The biomedical model focuses on mental *illness* or disease as measured by symptoms. In contrast, other schools of psychology focus on mental *health*, which is often equated with autonomy or freedom, including the capacity for rational choice and implying active involvement with others, authenticity, empathy, independence of thought, and courage (Cassimatis, 1979). Our theoretical and value preference is for a positive definition of mental health. In addition, we find it useful in the context of the present study to stress those aspects of mental health that should come to the fore in a personal crisis that call for an active response. Having adopted this position, we suggest the following questions concerning mental health needs other than the prevention of emotional disorders.

How many terminated workers will have the information and insight to assess realistically their personal situations? How many will actively seek information and new skills and resources in order to increase their chances of reemployment or to pursue other desired options? What explains variations in the efforts of workers to cope with job loss and variations in their success? Answers to these questions will have implications for the design of service programs aimed not only at the prevention of severe disorders in a minority but at improving the capacities and outcomes of the whole group of laid-off workers.

(F) *What have been the responses of mental health centers and other human services agencies to mass job loss?*

(G) *To the extent that these responses have been evaluated, what have been the results of such efforts?*

As noted above, there have been only a few documented community mental health programs focused on laid-off workers or the unemployed. In some instances, however, other human services agencies or coalitions of such agencies have attempted to deal with community unemployment crises. What have been the kinds of services and programs offered to workers? What has been the success of such efforts in reaching the unemployed and obtaining their participation? To the extent that systematic evaluations have been conducted, how appropriate and effective have these helping efforts been? Have other, less formal helping efforts been evident, and what have been their impacts?

(H) *Based on the evidence concerning both mental health needs and past responses to these needs, what mental health services and other public programs are most appropriate to deal with massive job losses?*

The ultimate goal of a policy-oriented analysis is to develop specific recommendations for programs and services. When are the most effective times to intervene? Can about-to-be-unemployed people be "inoculated" *en masse* against severe reactions and given better coping capacities through counseling and education? Can existing social networks or other informal channels be used to reach laid-off workers with information about services and to transmit information to human services agencies about people with emerging problems? What are the most effective means of identifying those at special risk and delivering them needed services? What combinations of services or other forms of assistance will be needed by people in various circumstances? How should services planning and delivery be organized and funded? What are the appropriate roles for community health centers, other local agencies and community leaders, and higher levels of government? How can we ensure that responses to mass unemployment are appropriately evaluated so that knowledge is cumulative?

These and similar questions can only be addressed once the preceding sets of questions have been at least tentatively answered. Even with answers to the entire list of questions, preventive programs directed at the unemployed cannot be implemented without facing other difficulties. These barriers, discussed below, affect the practicality of all prevention efforts in mental health, and, unless they are solved, prevention will be more a catchword than a reality.

BARRIERS TO IMPLEMENTATION

Whatever the state of our technical knowledge about prevention, actual implementation of such programs will require skill in dealing with conflicting values, conflicting interests, and a complex, often chaotic organizational environment.

(1) Ambiguous and conflicting goals. There is no consensus concerning the purposes and priorities of the community mental health program. In particular, and as noted earlier, there is disagreement about whether prevention programs should now or ever be a major part of community mental health services. But, even within the group that supports prevention as a priority, there are differences not just over what environmental factors are most damaging and which modalities are most appropriate but, more fundamentally, over the meaning of the goal. For instance, "primary prevention," which includes efforts to meet mental health problems stemming from job loss, can be subdivided into what Dooley and Catalano (1980) term "proactive primary" and "reactive primary prevention." These technical phrases may mask a deep-seated value conflict between those who seek to ameliorate and soften the effects of unregulated social or economic change (reactive primary) and others who believe that prevention requires much more radical action to purge the society of "the noxious or causal agent" (proactive primary) (Dooley & Catalano, 1980, p. 22). Obviously, such value conflicts reach well beyond the bounds of the community mental health programs; as a result, debates over mental health policies to deal with job loss become intertwined with broader arguments over the role of government and nature of society.

(2) The politics of community service delivery. On a more practical level, any new service program must be implemented in an environment of conflicting professional, agency, jurisdictional, and other political interests. Both within and beyond the community mental health movement, organized professional groups and adherents of differing clinical/ideological perspec-

tives are in conflict. Superimposed on these cleavages are "turf" disputes, stable or shifting electoral alliances, geography-based rivalries, and other continuing conflicts peculiar to a particular community. There will always be conflicts, manifest or latent, between human service needs and other public priorities; in communities experiencing major job losses, the struggle for shares of a shrinking budget may be especially sharp and painful. Finally, there will be "class" conflicts between advocates of services to established agency clienteles (often including the poor) and advocates of expanding services to new groups (including the newly unemployed). Such conflicts cannot be avoided, nor can they be easily managed.

(3) The organization of local service delivery. Apart from the value and interest conflicts to be dealt with, other practical problems stand in the way of effective service programs for the unemployed. As with other prevention programs, the obstacles to implementation include fragmentation of funding and responsibility; lack of coordination and communication among related service providers; and the weakness of mechanisms for planning, institutional learning, and program innovation. Although some states and communities have made strides toward better "services integration" (Polivka, Imershein, White, & Stivers, 1977), the prevailing pattern is complex and confusing—especially to those in need of help, but unused to dealing with formal agencies.

The lack of integrated services systems is a particular problem if effective treatment means treating people in varied circumstances; whose reactions to stress may manifest themselves in varied ways and at various times; and who typically require the services of more than one, often several, specialized agencies. The lack of services integration also implies having no centralized point of services access, information, and referral for people seeking help. It implies no unified diagnostic and tracking capacities. It also implies an absence of joint planning and evaluation. Finally, given the fragmented state of human services delivery in the United States, the authority necessary to assign and enforce agency responsibilities and cooperation is lacking. Thus, any interagency coordination of planning and programs will be almost totally voluntary.

CONCLUSION AND PLAN OF THE BOOK

This chapter has specified in some detail the intellectual and practical problems to be solved before effective preventive programs can be put in place to meet the mental health needs of people out of work. In doing so, it illustrates the difficulty of translating the ideal of prevention into appropriate services.

The next chapter reviews previous research on unemployment and job loss as well as evaluations of human services responses to these problems.

Some of the many questions not fully answered by previous studies are investigated in our own work, dealing with massive job losses in Youngstown, Ohio. The following four chapters describe and report findings from the Youngstown studies. Chapter 3 outlines their methodology. Chapter 4 presents statistical evidence on the level and distribution of stress reactions among affected workers. Chapter 5 presents a series of family case studies, illustrating the variety of personal responses to the crisis of job loss. In Chapter 6, the responses of the community mental health center and other local services agencies are described and evaluated.

The final chapters of the book present our best judgments regarding the mental health policies and programs appropriate to deal with the needs produced by massive job losses.

Chapter 2

THE KNOWLEDGE BASE
A Review of Recent Research

The research literature on mental health and the economy has
expanded rapidly in recent years. In this brief chapter, a review
of that literature is focused on the questions raised in Chapter 1.
One purpose of the literature review is to describe the current
knowledge base from which mental health policies for job loss
can be constructed. A complementary goal is to highlight gaps
or weaknesses in that knowledge base. The discussion parallels
that of the first chapter.

JOB LOSS AND STRESS

Three classes of empirical studies provides circumstantial
evidence that unemployment and/or accompanying hardships
contribute to social and psychological disorders. The first class
is made up of collected case studies of the unemployed and
profiles of families of the unemployed or of communities experiencing massive job losses and economic hardships. Several of
these studies date from the Depression era (Zawadski, Bohan,
& Lazarsfeld, 1935; Komarovsky, 1940; Bakke, 1940; Eisenberg & Lazarsfeld, 1938; Jahoda, 1979; Jahoda, Lazarsfeld, &

Ziesel, 1971). However, the tradition continues (Slote, 1969; Liebow, 1967; Strange, 1977; Maurer, 1979). Although limited as a research methodology, the ethnographic and case studies are invaluable for understanding the varied dynamics of human response to economic stresses; they continue to aid researchers by generating insights otherwise unavailable and by offering hypotheses for testing by other methods. The series of family portraits presented in Chapter 5 is in this tradition.

The second class of studies associating economic stress with mental or social disorders are cross-sectional analyses of the statistical relationships in a given population between measures of individual economic circumstances (including employment status) and indicators of social and psychological condition. Once again, there are many such studies (Dohrenwend & Dohrenwend, 1974; Caplovitz, 1979; Durham, 1976). The fruits of such work are very limited, since it can reveal little about the dynamics of disorder development or even the direction of causality between economic hardship and disorder. Also, the various measures of economic circumstances tend to be highly intercorrelated; thus, separate effects of unemployment are virtually impossible to assess by this method.

A third, more sophisticated class of empirical studies provides some compelling evidence that job loss and/or unemployment has been a major source of social disorders and individual mental dysfunction. Foremost among these are the studies of Harvey Brenner (1973, 1976) statistically relating multiyear variations in regional or national unemployment rates to fluctuations in aggregate indicators of social and personal disorder.[1] Brenner's work shows that increased mental hospital admissions, higher suicide rates, and higher rates of stress-related illnesses or behaviors have tended to follow increases in state or U.S. unemployment rates. These patterns have been consistent over several decades. Moreover, the relationships are of such a magnitude that unemployment is implicated as one of the major environmental sources of personal stress. At the same time, there is evidence that at least some groups (e.g., the poor and elderly) in the population are harmed by economic expansion or prosperity (Brenner, 1973; Eyer, 1977; Catalano & Dooley, 1979; Freudenburg, Bacigalupi, & Landoll-Young, 1982). Thus, the relationship between economic change and social stress is more complex than at first meets the eye.

The knowledge that unemployment is associated with stress is only a starting point. By their nature, the three classes of studies described above are limited in what they can reveal. Case studies suggest but cannot test hypotheses about the ways job losses may lead to stress and sometimes to emotional disorders. The aggregate statistical studies, on the other hand, shed little light on how or why these relationships have occurred. To obtain the more specific insights needed to guide mental health policy, it is necessary to follow groups of individuals through the experience of job loss and the subsequent period of unemployment. Also, the design preferably will include parallel tracking of still-employed groups that are otherwise similar to the laid-off groups.[2]

There is a need for many such studies, which should be conducted with varied populations: those laid off en masse as well as those fired; high-paid industrial workers and low-wage workers; unionized and nonunionized employees; white-collar, traditional blue-collar, and service workers; women and men; those in large labor markets and those in isolated communities; those laid off in prosperous times and those fired in hard times. We need to have studies of this design that have been continued over multiyear periods and have employed a range of measurement techniques. However, the number of such panel design studies to date is small.

The work of Cobb and Kasl (1977) is of particular interest, despite the small sample size, because of its sophisticated psychological and physiological measures. Another feature of this study design makes it potentially more useful than others: samples were drawn and measurements were made prior to plant closings and accompanying layoffs. As a result, Cobb and Kasl were able to gauge effects during an extended period when workers were still employed but anticipating termination. The researchers collected a great variety of information over a two-and-one-half year period, including health readings, questionnaire measures of mental health, and data on changes in economic circumstances. Parallel data were collected in plants not threatened with closure. Among many specific findings, the following are deserving of mention here (1977, pp. 174-182):

- For most, the experience of job loss is stressful, "involving about as much life change as getting married" and "requiring several months to return to normal" (p. 174).
- Job loss and/or subsequent unemployment were associated with increased depression, anomie, anger/irritation, suspicion, and other symptoms of psychological stress.
- The change in risk factors for coronary heart disease is such that an excess of such disease among terminated workers could be expected. Other physical problems that were significantly greater among the terminated groups were suicide, dyspepsia, joint swelling, hypertension, and alopecia.
- Self-reports of illness and drug use for acute conditions were high during the anticipation phase, dropped at termination, and rose again at six months.
- Those who were unemployed longer and had less social support experienced more stress.
- The length of time a person was unemployed was a predictor of health problems.

Cobb and Kasl are candid about the limits of their study. They believe, for instance, that the statistical measures of effective states and deprivation do not fully capture the degree of anguish experienced by the workers and their families (1977, p. 180). Another apparent limitation is the demographic composition of the sample, which was predominantly composed of white, middle-aged males.

Most other studies employing such quasi-experimental designs have produced results consistent with the above. The work to date is sufficient to justify concern over the health and mental health effects of job loss and unemployment.

TIMING AND SEQUENCE OF EFFECTS

Craig King (1982) has summarized findings from various studies regarding the phases of worker reaction to job loss (Eisenberg & Lazarsfeld, 1938; Powell & Driscoll, 1973; Slote, 1969; Taber, Walsh, & Cooke, 1979; Root, 1979). Some of the tentative conclusions derived from this work:

- Denial or disbelief is a typical initial response to rumors of termination.
- Considerable anxiety occurs during the period after a plant closing announcement, as rumors circulate and as layoffs begin.
- The several weeks after termination is a period of relaxation and relief, of optimism, and often of vigorous efforts to find a new job.
- During this period, friends and family give maximum social support.
- Four or more months after termination, those workers still unemployed go through a period of "vacillation and doubt"—in which *some* experience panic, rage, self-doubt, deep and potentially suicidal depression, erratic behavior, and interpersonal or marital problems (King, 1982, p. 70)— lasting from one to three months. This stage may be followed by a final period of "malaise and cynicism," in which mood stabilizes but apathy, listlessness, resignation, and fatalism increase (King, 1982; Powell & Driscoll, 1973).

The likelihood that a given individual will experience all of these stages obviously depends on the duration of unemployment.[3] Also, it is important to emphasize that these are generalizations and not the common experience of all unemployed persons. Differences of personality and circumstances influence both the timing and intensity of effects.

PEOPLE AT SPECIAL RISK

Job loss is a different experience for someone holding a first job than for someone near retirement, for white-collar as opposed to blue-collar workers, for those who were content in their jobs versus those who were not. The experience is likely to differ depending on personal employment history and on current personal resources and personality, as these affect the ability to cope with such shocks. Some of these variations are themselves a reflection of demography and group memberships: race or ethnicity, education, age, or other readily measured attributes. A number of studies have examined such relationships to determine what groups are at special risk of harm due to job loss (Braginsky & Braginsky, 1975; Powell & Driscoll, 1973; Cohn, 1978; Schlozman & Verba, 1979; Liem & Liem, 1979; Foltman, 1968).

One mental health crisis center has described its unemployed clients as falling into three distinct groups: (1) a large number of unemployable, chronically poor persons; (2) a smaller group of frequently unemployed, marginally adjusted people; and (3) an increasing number of persons with stable work records, interpersonal relations, and usually adequate coping abilities for whom job loss is a major change in the course of their lives (Rueth & Heller, 1981). These categories are useful because the loss of employment is, subjectively, a very different experience for people in each group. On the other hand, any mass termination, as in a plant closing, will affect people of widely varied work histories, social integration, and psychological condition. Thus typologies such as this cannot be used to predict individual response, and it is useful to examine variations within any group of unemployed persons.

Social support. A fairly consistent finding of these studies is that social support from friends or relatives tends to mitigate the harmful effects of such shocks as job loss (Core, 1978; Cobb, 1976; Dean & Lin, 1977; Kaplan, Cassell, & Core, 1977). Liem and Liem (1979, p. 350) have also reviewed such research and conclude that evidence for the mitigating effects of social support is "often mixed, and . . . is frequently open to alternative interpretations." They note that social support may itself be eroded by prolonged unemployment. Liem and Liem also argue the need for more detailed study of the ways in which different categories of friends, relatives, and other associates may offer specific kinds of help to the unemployed. Such process studies could be particularly useful in designing formal interventions.

The family. The family is a special case of social support. The natural support structure of immediate and extended families may buoy up the unemployed in a variety of ways: with other members offering helpful information and comfort; with material help; by decreased consumption; or by themselves taking jobs to provide alternative income to the household. On the other hand, an unemployed breadwinner may not always welcome such assistance. Rayman (1982) has found that unemployed men are more likely to seek help from their spouses; whereas, women more often turn to other family members and friends. She also notes that women tend more than men to maintain connections with their former coworkers and to form informal support groups.

Although study results are not completely consistent, there is reason to believe that single persons; newcomers to a community; those isolated from strong ethnic, religious, or other group memberships; and others without access to social support are at special risk following loss of employment. Second, there is some evidence that prolonged unemployment weakens family and other personal relations and, consequently, reduces the mitigating effects of such relationships (Liem & Liem, 1979; Furstenberg, 1974; Levin, 1975). On this point, however, the evidence is less consistent (Jacobson, 1977). Certainly, job loss changes both the pattern and quality of a person's interactions with others. Contact with some friends may be lost, while some old relationships take on new importance as sources of aid and comfort. Some apparently healthy marriages may break up under these stresses, while others are strengthened. In short, the interplay of effects between job loss and social support can be complex.

Race and ethnicity. Racial and ethnic background have been and continue to be important determinants of social experience and influences on economic opportunity. Racial and cultural differences may interact with job loss to either increase or decrease its harmful effects. We suspect this is the case for two reasons. First, historical hiring practices tend to produce racial and ethnic or language group predominance in certain work groups or occupations. In the steel industry, for instance, race/ethnicity status overlays work roles to produce complex informal patterns of social status and relationship within the mill (Kornblum, 1974). Following a plant closing, racial or ethnic group ties among former workers may be the basis for social support and exchange of communications (Rayman, 1982, p. 329). Unfortunately, no studies have fully explored the influence that ethnic group memberships have on stress reactions or coping behavior following job loss.

Second, race continues to be an important determinant of job opportunity, due in part at least to past and present racial discrimination. Squires notes that

> among workers who lose their jobs, minorities encounter greater difficulties in securing new positions, as is indicated by the fact that the average duration of unemployment for whites during the fourth quarter of 1979 was just five weeks compared to 7.1 weeks for non-whites [1981, p. 13].

In every U.S. economic downturn, blacks suffer more economic hardship than others. They are more likely to exhaust personal and family financial resources. Statistically, their average economic status declines relative to that of white Americans. On a micro-level, black and Hispanic workers losing jobs are likely to be at a disadvantage in one or more of the following ways: (1) given the recency of affirmative action efforts, they may have less average seniority and, therefore, fewer rights and benefits; (2) they may be concentrated in low-pay, lower skill positions that have provided them with job experience for which there is less demand among prospective employers; (3) they may have received poorer education or training; and (4) they may experience difficulty in finding new employment that derives either from direct discrimination or institutional barriers that relate indirectly to past or present discrimination (housing patterns, flows of information about job opportunities, and so on). However, very few studies have systematically considered the interaction between job loss and race.

Age and education. Various other personal characteristics may be correlated with responses to job loss. These include age and education. Older workers tend to have less formal education; what education or training they possess often is less relevant to their prospects for reemployment than are the skills they have acquired through work experience. The specialized skills of older workers are sometimes less transferable to other work settings or industries than the "portable" education credentials of younger workers. Age is also related to other factors that shape the job loss experience, including seniority and associated bumping or transfer rights; eligibility for early retirement; "breadwinner" status and family obligations; and age discrimination. Thus, there is ample reason to examine how both age and education influence the effects of job loss.

There is some evidence that middle-aged and older workers may suffer more psychological stress than younger persons from job loss (Kasl, Gore, & Cobb, 1975; Sheppard, 1965). Haber, Ferman, and Hudson (1936) reviewed seventeen studies that dealt with the interaction between job loss and age; in thirteen, older displaced workers were found more likely to experience prolonged unemployment. Advanced age was usually combined with less formal education. Later studies by Foltman (1968), Lipsky (1970), and Strange (1977) all support this generalization.

Longer range and secondary effects. Although the impact of job loss is limited at first to those directly affected and their families, the well-being of others may sooner or later be jeopardized. In the near term, massive layoffs heighten competition for work in the labor market area; thus, the risk of unemployment increases for less experienced and less educated job seekers. In this way, a substantial proportion of the unemployment burden may be shifted from the first wave of terminated workers to the least competitive fraction of the region's potential labor force. Even longer term impacts may spread to children through changes in early life experience that flow from a parent's unemployment. It is also possible that over many years, a series of economic setbacks can permanently change the social and cultural patterns of a community or region.

The few statistical studies of how entire communities may be affected by a major closing have so far focused on only the first two or three years following such events (Gold, 1981; Weeks & Drengacz, 1982; Hansen et al., 1980).

One long-term study by Elder and Rockwell (1979) associates fathers' persistent economic hardships occurring during the Depression years with decreased chances of completing college among their sons and daughters in the 1950s. Also of some interest is a series of studies that describe the development of a subculture in Appalachia associated with rural poverty, isolation, and economic dependency (Caudill, 1963) and invoke this culture as a factor explaining reactions to job losses in the region (Strange, 1977; Field, Ewing, & Wayne, 1957; Williams, Foltman, & Rosen, n.d.; Cook, 1967). It appears that this culture has discouraged risk-taking, job-seeking, and mobility among terminated workers.

EVIDENCE OF COPING BEHAVIOR

The focus of most studies cited above has been on negative consequences of stress, including evidence of emotional disorders. However, a broader concern for the mental health implications of job loss leads to questions about the range of coping behaviors and their success. In other words, it is important to know to what extent terminated workers adopt active, creative strategies for dealing with job loss or reducing its harmful effects on themselves and their families. It is also important to examine what personal or environmental factors promote or discourage appropriate coping behavior.

Some studies suggest that many recently unemployed people use only limited or unimaginative means of adapting to their situations (King, 1982). Schlozman and Verba (1979) conclude that, even in an era of generous unemployment benefits, households of the unemployed do experience hardship and typically respond by cutting back on expenditures and seeking new sources of income or material resources.

Other important forms of coping are retraining and job search. Although retraining is usually of limited short-run value in securing new employment (Schultz & Weber, 1966; Stern, 1973; Pursell et al., 1975; Samuelson, 1981; Hansen et al., 1980), it may have other benefits. Retraining provides a constructive use of leisure time, helps maintain social contacts, and in many instances, is tied to extension of the unemployment compensation period. Job searching is obviously a key method of attempted adjustment. Research has shown that both the level and efficiency of searching varies enormously from person to person. Many studies have also shown that the overwhelming number of job placements result from informal contacts and referrals and from self-initiated applications rather than from information or referrals provided by public employment agencies (Thompson, 1965; Wilcock & Ranke, 1963; Blau, 1964; Foltman, 1968). Bendick and Devine (1981) have found that workers displaced by economic change are slower than other less experienced workers in finding new employment; their reemployment may be slowed by such handicaps as home ownership, the expectation of wages and fringe benefits comparable to those of previous jobs, and high total family income relative to other unemployed persons. Such workers are also less likely than others to move in search of jobs. Of course, finding a new job does not always resolve the problems of those displaced from well-paying and otherwise attractive jobs; often the new job is unstable, financially unrewarding, and less satisfactory in other ways than previous employment (Wilcock & Franke, 1963; Schlozman & Verba, 1979). The "informal economy" is a not easily measured mechanism for helping some households generate replacement income and for bartering (Jahoda, 1979; Dow, 1977).

A less attractive form of adaptive behavior has been documented by some studies: adoption of the "sick role" (Strange, 1977; Segall, 1976). Another frequently measured coping method is increased alcohol consumption (Brenner, 1975; Pearlin & Radabaugh, 1976; LeMasters, 1975; Weeks & Drengacz, 1982; King, 1982). As previously noted, there apparently tends to be a deterioration of coping capacity among those still unemployed after several months. However, to date, few studies have carefully examined how and why coping responses vary so widely within groups of terminated workers.

FORMAL RESPONSES TO JOB LOSS

Systematic observations of how mental health centers and other organizations address job loss are few because programs to meet the needs of newly unemployed people are few. On the other hand, some conceptual work has been done that is useful in classifying the range of possible responses according to when and how they address the problem.

In the first category is a report on formation of a community services council following a major plant closing (Taber, Walsh, & Cooke, 1979). Taber and his colleagues assisted community decision-makers in planning and organizing a coordinated response by manpower, education, financial, health, and recreation agencies. Although not formally evaluated, the effort appears to have been successful in assessing worker needs and making referrals. Another similar planning effort in Youngstown, Ohio was unsuccessful in affecting agency programs or increasing interagency cooperation (Buss & Redburn, 1980). This effort revealed that a lack of incentives and substantial obstacles discourage effective human service responses to plant closings or similar events; although the planning group was able to agree on a number of specific service needs, no agency had clear responsibility for any of the programs thus identified.

A 1980 survey of social services administrators in Hartford, Connecticut—a city where aircraft industry employment had dropped from 80,000 to 47,000 workers and where black youth unemployment then exceeded fifty percent—found that "mental health administrators, alcohol treatment center personnel, employment and training personnel, and church leaders demonstrated that minimal consciousness seems to exist in human services regarding the problems of the unemployed" (Rayman, 1982, p. 330). Also, "except for one inner-city priest, one alcohol treatment administrator, and one ex-aircraft worker, who acted as a liaison to organized labor . . . no social services respondent knew of programs particularly earmarked for the unemployed" (p. 330). More hopefully, this study reported that a United Way-sponsored United Labor Center was being launched to form emergency referral and outreach offices when and where future layoffs or closings occurred.

Catalano and Dooley's (1980) classification scheme divides preventive interventions into these groups:

(1) *Proactive primary:* efforts to reduce or avoid the risk factor (e.g., job loss);
(2) *Reactive primary:* efforts to improve coping and adaptation among people exposed to the risk factors; and
(3) *Secondary:* detection and treatment of early symptoms of disorder to prevent further damage.

Examples of proactive primary prevention efforts at a macro level would include legislation aimed at guaranteeing employment or action to forestall a pending plant closing. On a similar scale, proactive primary prevention might be realized through prelayoff counseling that increased the efficiency of job search or other individual coping responses. The national Humphrey-Hawkins legislation and certain recommendations of the National Commission for Employment Policy are perhaps the closest the United States has come to a national policy of pro-active primary prevention regarding structural unemployment or midcareer job loss. Recently, some have suggested that the social costs of economic change be explicitly calculated and considered when regional or national economic policies are formulated or when corporations decide to close major operations (Dooley & Catalano, 1980; Beck-Rex, 1978). On a plant or community level, there are some largely unevaluated examples of "early warning" or "stress inoculation" efforts in advance of a plant closing. Stone and Kieffer (1981) have developed an approach to prelayoff intervention based on their experience with job loss effects in a Detroit-area mental health center. The British Steel Corporation has cooperated with local authorities in providing prelayoff counseling as well as later follow-up assistance to workers idled by steel mill closings. Also, a few U.S. corporations have mounted similar efforts (Commerce-Labor Adjustment Action Committee, 1979; Stern, 1973). Early warning of a plant closing may be essential to the implementation of prelayoff programs. Some states and communities have developed formal mechanisms to meet this need (Nathanson, 1980).

Work addressing the problem of what human service programs are needed to deal with job losses, or how they are to be designed and implemented, is virtually nonexistent. The few helping efforts cited above have not been systematically evaluated. Consequently, the policy suggestions that have been made draw either on personal experience or deductions from research on job loss impacts and mediating factors. Liem and Liem (1979), for instance, have emphasized the role of social support and naturally occurring social networks as possible means of promoting successful adjustment (see also Hirsh,

1980). However, these observations are no substitute for action research aimed at developing and assessing new programs or for formal evaluation of communities' human services responses to economic crises.

Summary:
What We Do and Do Not Know

The knowledge base for a community mental health response to job loss is strongest in demonstrating the general need for such programs. It is also helpful in identifying some personal or environmental factors that increase the probability that loss of work will produce damaging levels of stress. Nevertheless, many gaps in the literature make it an inadequate basis for policy development; others have reached similar conclusions (Gordus, 1979; King, 1982). There are very few studies of:

- women workers and minority workers;
- family responses, especially effects on children's education and later careers;
- the impact of job losses on community social institutions; and
- the longer range effects of job loss.

Other gaps related to the dynamics or etiology of stress reactions and disorders connected with job loss. There is

- little information on how personality predisposes reactions to job loss;
- too little detail on the kinds of social support and institutional arrangements most helpful to successful adaptation;
- inadequate understanding of why job search efficiency and other coping responses vary so greatly from person to person; and
- inadequate understanding of how the initial round of effects spreads or is displaced to others in the labor market or community.

However, the widest gaps in our knowledge concern the kinds of formal programs or other responses that will be effective in either preventing mental illness or enhancing adaptation following job loss. There are

- no demonstrations of what interventions are effective at various stages and with various types of individuals;
- few studies of the practical barriers to integrated planning and programming to deal with economic crisis; and
- few studies of service utilization or access that are directly relevant to job loss.

In short, there are still many questions to be answered before mental health programming is grounded in adequate knowledge about the problem and how to deal with it. The Youngstown studies described in the following chapters were designed with these gaps in mind. They provide the first systematic answers to some of the questions raised in this and the preceding chapter.

Notes

1. Careful methodological critiques of Brenner have been conducted by Barling and Handel (1980) and Catalano and Dooley (1979).

2. Dooley and Catalano (1980) have agreed that "an ideal study would include randomly assigned control and experimental groups and an independent economic group, and an independent economic variable controlled by the experimenter." However, we are skeptical about whether such studies, even assuming that ethical and practical barriers were surmounted, could shed much light on the effects of job losses as they occur in a natural, that is, uncontrolled setting.

3. Wright Bakke (1940) offers a somewhat different, six-phase model of adjustment, beginning with initial shock and anger and ending with "permanent readjustment" characterized by a willingness to accept lower paying work in order to restore stable income.

Chapter 3

THE YOUNGSTOWN STUDIES

The Youngstown studies were undertaken to provide new information useful in constructing appropriate public policies for mass unemployment of industrial workers. One major focus was on how workers and their families reacted to job loss and how these responses translated into mental health needs. A second focus was on the responses of formal (public and private) agencies and institutions to this type of community crisis; particular attention was given to the actions and programs of community mental centers and other human service agencies. By combining these two, it is possible to judge the appropriateness of agency responses to the demonstrated needs of workers and families. This leads, in turn, to propositions about what would be effective preventive mental health programs for meeting needs generated by massive job losses.

The Youngstown research began with the sudden announcement, in September 1977, that the Lykes Corporation would immediately close the Campbell Works of its giant steel-making subsidiary, Youngstown Sheet and Tube Company. Initially, nearly 4,100 workers were laid off; hundreds more would follow. A longitudinal panel study design was chosen so that groups of terminated and continuously employed workers and their families could be observed over an extended period.

In this respect, it is similar to Kasl and Cobb's (1979) research. However, it was decided that survey research techniques were preferable to the intensive and costly clinicial and physiological measurements employed in their studies. This choice was as much a function of limited resources as of research objectives. With regard to the latter, if was decided that less intensive study of various categories of workers, as well as their spouses and children, would better serve the policy focus of the research. At the same time, researchers began to monitor implementation of mental health programs for the newly unemployed, supported by an emergency grant from the Ohio Department of Mental Health, and began to track other local agency responses to the employment crisis.

In this chapter, the methods and methodological problems of the Youngstown studies are outlined with two purposes in mind. First, readers should know enough about the research methods used so that they can reach their own judgments about the credibility of findings and policy conclusions drawn from them. Second, a frank discussion of methodology is useful to others who may want to conduct similar studies and add further to the knowledge base for mental health policy development.

Findings in this study concerning the mental health effects of massive layoffs are based on detailed personal interviews with steelworkers and managers from Youngstown Sheet and Tube Company and from members of their families where appropriate. Steelworkers and managers whose jobs were terminated constituted one treatment group. The spouses and children and those laid off constituted a second treatment group. Steelworkers and managers from Sheet and Tube whose jobs appeared to be secure at the time of the study made up one comparison group. Correspondingly, their spouses and children made up a second comparison group.

Personal interviews were completed one (summer 1978) and two (summer 1979) years after the steel mill closing announcement in September 1977. This allowed for some longitudinal comparisons of possible effects. By correlating responses from

Table 3.1   Sample Sizes for Selected Groups

Sample	First Wave Summer 1978	Second Wave Summer 1979
Steelworkers	273	150
Steelworker's Spouses	215	113
Steelworker's Children	100	NA
Managers	55	29
Manager's Spouses	39	20
Manager's Children	15	NA

the above groups to identical survey questions, it was possible to follow the impact of the crisis over time and note differences between groups.

In the sections that follow, the sample design, sample characteristics, interview procedures, test instruments, and reliability/validity analyses are discussed.

SAMPLE DESIGN

Panel Study Design

Personal interviews were conducted in a panel study in two waves. Respondents were selected from probability samples designed to be representative of their respective groups. The first wave of interviews was conducted with employed and laid-off steelworkers and managers and their families during July and August 1978. Steelworkers were those who were union members, hourly employees, and who worked in the steel production process. Managers were those white-collar workers who were retained on salary.

As shown in Table 3.1, 273 steelworkers and 55 managers were interviewed. Some 215 spouses of steelworkers and 39 spouses of managers were interviewed. Also, 100 children of steelworkers and 15 children of managers were interviewed.

The second wave of interviews was conducted with respondents during July and August 1979. Respondents in the first

Table 3.2   Sample Sizes for Minority and College Scholarship Students

Sample	First Wave Summer 1978	Second Wave Summer 1979	Third Wave Spring 1981
Black Steelworkers	50	29	74
Treatment group	50	29	15
Control group	NA*	NA	59
Ethnic Steelworkers	35	21	56
Treatment group	35	21	24
Control group	NA	NA	32
College Students	NA	NA	132
Treatment group	NA	NA	77
Control group	NA	NA	55

*Indicates that no interviews were conducted.

wave were located and reinterviewed where possible. No substitutions of other respondents were made for people who could not be interviewed on the second wave. Table 3.1 shows that interviewers were able to complete second-wave interviews with 150 steelworkers and 29 managers, as well as with 113 steelworkers' spouses and 20 managers' spouses. Children were not reinterviewed.[1]

Minority Worker Subsamples

Minority workers—including blacks, who may experience racial discrimination, as well as Americans of European background who may be culturally or socially isolated or distinctive because of ethnicity or language—may have special problems as a result of plant closings. During spring 1981, an additional set of personal interviews was conducted with minority steelworkers from the first and second waves. At the same time, interviews were conducted with a new probability sample of minority steelworkers from other steel mills in the area.[2] This latter group served as a comparison group for analyses focusing on the special problems of minority workers.

Table 3.2 shows the minority worker sample sizes: 50 black steelworkers were interviewed on the first wave. Follow-up interviews were completed with 29 blacks on the second wave and 15 in spring 1981. Interviews with 59 other blacks, on the third wave only, constituted a comparison group.

Interviews with European ethnic minorities included 35 workers on the first wave, with follow-up interviews with 21 workers on the second and 24 on the third. Interviews with 32 workers constituted a control group for the third wave. Workers classified as ethnic minorities occurred naturally in the sample.

College Student Subsample

Young people may also be affected over time following a plant closing. Personal interviews were conducted with 77 college-age children of laid-off steelworkers and managers who were attending Youngstown State University (YSU) under special scholarships any time during the four years following the closing of the steel mills. A comparison group of 55 YSU students was also interviewed.

Approximately 187 students received special scholarships. Personal interviews were attempted with 187 students and completed with 77. Those who could not be interviewed in person were contacted by telephone to determine where they lived and what had happened to them once they left YSU. Some 64 telephone interviews of this kind were completed.

Explaining Second-Wave Response Rates

As indicated in Chapter 2, the type of longitudinal or panel research design employed in the Youngstown studies has clear advantages for analyzing the impacts of job loss. However, one weakness of a panel design is the inevitable loss of respondents after the first wave, especially when respondents have had their lives disrupted. The reasons why 123 of the original sample of 273 first-wave respondents could not be reinterviewed should be identified for two reasons: (1) to assess potential bias due to selective attrition; and (2) perhaps to shed light on the mobility and coping behavior of the terminated workers. Some 20 of these steelworkers migrated from the Youngstown area in search of jobs elsewhere. The fact that so few workers left the area is consistent with findings from other studies (e.g., Foltman, 1968; Aiken, Ferman, & Sheppard, 1968), which indicated that workers in distressed communities are unlikely to leave in great numbers, at least in the short term. Several explanations for this are evident: First, workers may be strongly tied to their communities; they may have friends and relatives nearby, children in school, mortgages on homes or automobiles, and so on. Second, they may believe that jobs in other communities are not available or will be difficult to locate. Third, workers may lack the financial resources to relocate. Fourth, many may believe that their old jobs will be reestablished or that new jobs can be found in the community.

Unhappily, two workers died during the course of the study. Both workers were near retirement age. It is not known what role, if any, forced, early retirement may have played in their deaths.

A large number of workers, thirty, found new jobs nearby, but for a variety of reasons could not be interviewed. Some of these workers were able to secure steel production jobs in Lorain and Warren, Ohio, as well as in Aliquippa, Pittsburgh, and Sharon, Pennsylvania. Because of commuting time of up to one and one-half hours and work schedules that varied from day to night shifts, it was impossible to arrange interviews with these workers.

A similarly large number of workers, thirty, declined to be interviewed on the second wave. Frequently, in explaining their refusals, they expressed the belief that the government, union, or corporation had betrayed them, that they were laid off through no fault of their own, and that efforts to recreate old jobs or generate new ones were insufficient. Our impression is that many in this group were experiencing various symptoms of emotional distress, although systematic study of their responses was impossible. Several letters of appeal and telephone pleas failed to persuade this group to participate in this round of interviews.

Table 3.3   Employment Status First and Second Waves
for Steelworkers and Managers

Employment Status	Steelworkers				Managers			
	First Wave		Second Wave		First Wave		Second Wave	
Employed	47%	128	48%	72	57%	29	59%	17
Unemployed	22	60	23	34	6	3	10	3
Rehired	19	51	17	26	22	11	21	6
Retired	12	34	12	18	16	8	10	3
Total	100	273	100	150	101	51*	100	29

*Four managers could not be classified.

In the spring of 1981, minority workers were reinterviewed in a third wave. Interviewers were able to reinterview 15 workers (all minority) of the 123 who were not interviewed in the second wave. These were about evenly divided between those who were commuting and those who refused to be interviewed in the second wave.

SAMPLE CHARACTERISTICS

Employment Status

For purposes of this analysis, respondents were separated into four groups. Respondents who were laid off were in one of three categories: *unemployed,* those who had no job at the time of the interview; *retired,* those who were eligible and chose to retire earlier than they would have had the steel mills remained open; and *rehired,* those who had been laid off, and at the time of the interview, had found new jobs to replace those lost. *Employed* respondents were those who worked for Sheet and Tube and were not laid off; this is the comparison group.

Table 3.3 shows the percentage breakdowns on employment status for steelworkers and managers on the first-wave interviews. Nearly one year following the closing, about half of the steelworkers and managers were still employed at some Sheet and Tube facility in the area. Other steelworkers and managers appeared to have found jobs to replace those lost (about one-fifth) or chose to retire early (less than one-fifth). Steelworkers were more likely to be unemployed (22%) than were managers (6%), one year following closing. These findings are consistent with others that suggest that white-collar workers have a wider variety of employment options to choose from than do specially skilled or unskilled blue-collar workers. As a result, they are able to make transitions from one job to another more readily (e.g., Foltman, 1968).

Potential Bias in the Second Wave

One concern in the study is that the dropouts in the second wave of interviews are not biasing the representativeness of the sample. Several statistical tests were conducted to test for this kind of bias. One of these is reported in Table 3.3. We looked at the employment status of individual workers in the first wave. If workers were reinterviewed in some biased way, the second wave employment status should be different than the first wave. Table 3.3 shows that nearly identical proportions of workers of each first wave employment status group remained in the first and second waves. Tests of this kind enhanced our confidence that both the first and second waves were representative of workers at Sheet and Tube.

Changes in Employment Status

The employment statuses of laid-off workers are not stable. Some workers remain unemployed, but many are hired at other jobs or are called back to their old jobs at least for short periods and sometimes more than once. To examine changes in employment status, a worker's employment status on the first wave was paired against his employment status on the second.

Results of the analysis in Table 3.4 show the wide variety of employment changes experienced by workers. About one-third (36%) of the steelworkers and two-fifths (43%) of the managers

Table 3.4   Transition in Employment Status from the First
to Second Wave for Steelworkers and Managers

Employment Status First Wave	Employment Status Second Wave			
	Employed	Unemployed	Rehired	Retired
Steelworkers				
Employed	36% 54	2% 3	7% 10	3% 5
Unemployed	2 3	7 10	15 22	NA*
Rehired	15 23	1 1	1 2	NA
Retired	1 1	3 4	3 4	5 8
Managers				
Employed	43% 12	NA	18% 5	NA
Unemployed	4 1	NA	4 1	NA
Rehired	14 4	4% 1	4 1	NA
Retired	7 2	NA	NA	4% 1

*Indicates that no cases of this type were observed.

were still employed at Sheet and Tube two years following the closing. At the other extreme, only seven percent of the steelworkers and none of the managers were unemployed after two years. Surprisingly, a large number of steelworkers (15%) and managers (14%) gave up new jobs they had secured to return to jobs at Sheet and Tube.

Among both the steelworkers and managers, nearly all in our sample were able to find jobs within two years.[3] There are several reasons for this. First, employment at the General Motors Lordstown Plant, some twenty miles from Youngstown, was expanding from 1977 to 1979. As a result, skilled workers were in great demand. Many steelworkers eventually found their way to Lordstown. Second, not all steel producers in the region were performing poorly. Indeed, many highly skilled, experienced workers were absorbed into steel mills in and around Youngstown. Third, many steelworkers have construction-related skills (e.g., carpentry, plumbing, brick laying, welding, and the like). Some of these workers were hired in the local construction industry. Fourth, most steel-workers appeared to have found jobs in less prestigious and lower paying occupations, especially service industries.

In spite of the apparent good fortune of many workers in securing jobs following the closing, their new jobs were often insecure. The General Motors Lordstown Plant and its sister plant, Packard Electric, have placed thousands of workers on permanent furlough. The Brier Hill Works, formerly of Youngs-town Sheet and Tube and now of Jones and Laughlin Steel Cor-poration, shut down in 1980, idling some 1,500 workers. U.S. Steel, during this period, permanently shut down its Youngs-town and McDonald Works, terminating the jobs of another 3,500 workers. Republic Steel has laid off over a thousand workers in its Campbell facility. The construction industry over the last year has virtually ceased operation in the area. Unemployment (as of March 1983) appears chronically set at twenty percent for the area, and nearly ten percent of the residents of Mahoning County are receiving some form of welfare assistance.

Minorities and Employment Status

A major concern of our study is the interaction of job loss with race or ethnicity. In Table 3.5, worker employment status is examined for nonminorities, blacks, and ethnics across the three waves of the study.

Table 3.5 shows that the employment status of steelworkers by race or ethnicity, of the first wave, made little difference. Nearly half of all three racial/ethnic groups remained employed at Sheet and Tube, about one-fifth were either employed or rehired in new jobs, and the remainder chose early retirement. Among steelworkers, therefore, there is no evidence that minority status was a factor in obtaining new jobs.[4]

Again, our concern is to determine whether our sample in the second wave is representative of the populations under study. Table 3.5 shows that nearly all employment categories by race or ethnicity remained stable from the first wave of interviews to the second.

Table 3.5   Race and Employment Status for Steelworkers
and Managers on the First and Second Waves,
With Third Wave Minority Interviews

Race/Employment Status	First Wave Spring 1978		Second Wave Summer 1979		Minority Samples Spring 1981	
Steelworkers						
Whites	100%	188	100%	100	NA*	
Employed	45	85	50	50	NA	
Unemployed	21	40	20	20	NA	
Rehired	20	37	18	18	NA	
Retired	14	26	12	12	NA	
Blacks	100	50	100	31	100%	74
Employed	44	22	35	11	23	17
Unemployed	24	12	29	9	27	20
Rehired	22	11	26	8	18	13
Retired	10	5	10	3	32	24
European Ethnics	100	35	100	21	100	56
Employed	60	21	57	12	46	26
Unemployed	23	8	24	5	20	11
Rehired	9	3	10	2	21	12
Retired	9	3	10	2	13	7
Managers						
Whites	100%	48	100%	33	NA	
Employed	60	29	52	17	NA	
Unemployed	6	3	9	3	NA	
Rehired	23	11	18	6	NA	
Retired	10	5	21	7	NA	
Blacks	100	2	100	1	NA	
Employed	100	2	0	0	NA	
Unemployed	0	0	0	0	NA	
Rehired	0	0	0	0	NA	
Retired	0	0	100	1	NA	
European Ethnics	1000	0	100	0	NA	

*Indicates that no interviews were conducted.

The representativeness of third wave data (also in Table
3.5) is more difficult to establish. This is true because: (1)

after four years, the number of workers still in the original sample has decreased; (2) the minority subsample sizes are small as a result; (3) there exists no comparison group of nonminority workers; and (4) minorities may have undergone extensive employment status changes during a four-year period. In spite of these difficulties, there remains the possibility of comparing aggregate data for minority groups over time.

Even though there are insufficient numbers of workers in different categories to make inferences about minority populations, the changes in employment status through which minority groups passed during the course of our four-year study are revealing. In all, some 64 possible patterns could describe changes in employment status over three waves. That is, if there are four categories to which a worker may be assigned—employed, unemployed, rehired, and retired—then at the time of the second wave, the worker may have experienced 1 of 16 combinations ($4 \times 4 = 16$). By the third wave, some 64 combinations are possible ($4 \times 4 \times 4 = 64$). Clearly, our sample is not large enough to have even one representative among minority groups in each of the 64 combinations. Table 3.6 shows the change in employment status among minority workers for which data were available.

Table 3.6 shows that nearly one-fourth of the workers were continuously employed at Sheet and Tube. The remaining three-fourths, however, experienced a wide variety of changes in employment status, with no particular pattern of change dominating the others. Importantly, we have only concerned ourselves with three points in time. The shift in employment status may have been even more chaotic for some workers. Even when thousands of workers are laid off, then, individuals may still experience relatively unique circumstances.

From a methodological perspective, this poses major problems in determining how to assign workers to employment categories, since any control of this kind will greatly mask individual differences. At the same time, failure to collapse categories defies any sort of group analysis. We have elected to

Table 3.6   Changes in Employment Status for Minority Workers
in the First, Second, and Third Waves

	Employment Status		
Number of Workers	First Wave Summer 1978	Second Wave Summer 1979	Minority Sample Spring 1981
3	Unemployed ———	Unemployed ———	Unemployed
2	Unemployed ———	Rehired ———	Unemployed
1	Rehired ———	Employed ———	Unemployed
1	Employed ———	Employed ———	Unemployed
1	Rehired ———	Unemployed ———	Retired
1	Employed ———	Retired ———	Retired
1	Unemployed ———	Retired ———	Retired
2	Retired ———	Retired ———	Retired
2	Employed ———	Employed ———	Retired
1	Employed ———	Employed ———	Rehired
2	Retired ———	Rehired ———	Employed
1	Rehired ———	Rehired ———	Employed
12	Employed ———	Employed ———	Employed
1	Rehired ———	Not interviewed ———	Retired
2	Employed ———	Not interviewed ———	Retired
5	Employed ———	Not interviewed ———	Rehired
2	Rehired ———	Not interviewed ———	Employed
40 Total			

deal with employment status as an indicator only for one of three discrete time periods.

Age and Education

Age and education are important factors in describing a sample. Table 3.7 shows the age and education breakdowns for steelworkers in the study.

Table 3.7 reveals that workers fall naturally into two age groups: younger (less than 24 years old) and older (55 years old or older), with older workers predominating. This pattern is consistent with conventional wisdom about the steel industry: its workers tend to be older. One major reason for this phenomenon is that younger workers typically are lower in seniority

Table 3.7   Age and Education of Steelworkers on the First
            and Second Waves (in Percentages)

Age/Education	First Wave	Second Wave
Age (years)		
less than 24	22	24
25 to 34	8	9
35 to 44	9	11
45 to 54	14	32
55 and older	44	8
not reported	13	15
Total	100	100
	(273)	(150)
Education		
grade school	11	7
some high school	18	17
high school[a]	34	32
some college	18	19
college	4	5
not reported	16	17
Total	101[b]	98[b]
	(273)	(150)

a. Indicates high school, trade school, and vocational/technical education.
b. Does not total 100% due to rounding error.

and are, therefore, laid off first. Over the last two decades, the recurrent layoffs of workers may have discouraged younger workers from seeking continued employment in the industry. In addition, attitudes about making steel may be changing. Workers in our study overwhelmingly (three-fourths) reported that they would not like their children to become steelworkers. Most would like a professional career for their offspring. Consequently, the tradition of entire families working in the mills may be changing. Data for managers paralleled exactly that for steelworkers.[5]

Education levels for steelworkers were also consistent with expectations for the industry. The average steelworker has slightly less than a high school education. Most of those with lower levels of education are older workers. Twenty or thirty years ago when they entered the steel mills, high levels of formal education were not required or even in many cases particularly useful. Workers obtained jobs either by knowing someone in the mills or by having a good work record. Younger workers seem to have different expectations. For them, the mills are a means to an end: The high wages in the mills and sometimes flexible working hours offer them an opportunity to increase their education ultimately to get out of the mills. Managers, as might be expected, are much more educated than steelworkers. Their education level averages just below a completed college degree.[6]

Again, we included second-wave data on age and education levels to ensure that our samples were representative. Table 3.7 shows that steelworker data for the first and second waves are nearly identical. Data for managers paralleled the findings for steelworkers.[7]

Interview Procedure

Interviews averaging two hours were conducted by an experienced, well-trained staff in the homes of workers. Each respondent was isolated and interviewed separately.[8]

Methodological Orientation of the Study

We have conducted our study using a social/psychological conception of mental health. Several caveats about our methodology must be mentioned. First, since we were not dealing with a medical model perspective, we did not use standard pathology-seeking diagnostic test instruments (e.g., Warheit, Holzer, Robbins, & Buhl, 1979). Therefore, although we might offer *some* evidence concerning two forms of depression (see dimensional analysis below) as indicative of psychopathological problems, we cannot provide a more holistic problem interpretation. We also cannot validate our study based upon our diagnostic instruments, since they would at best only constitute a meager set of items on the more elaborate instruments such as the Minnesota Multiphasic Personality Inventory (MMPI).

Second, we did not employ clinical psychologists or psychiatrists as interviewers. We chose to use survey researchers in face-to-face contact with respondents. We cannot, then, offer clinical evaluation data on any of the respondents that a mental health professional could have provided.

Third, without standardized tests or clinical evaluations, we could not make inferences about our findings concerning the general public of normals or abnormals. This would not be consistent with our social-psychological perspective. We did not feel that the principal research task of our study was to compare the mental health of different groups in our study with the mental health of the general population. Instead, we sought to compare workers and their spouses who were affected to various degrees with workers unaffected by the closing of the steel mills. We are able to assess changes in mental health of workers and their spouses.

The focus on the social psychological perspective of mental health does not imply that our perspective is to be preferred over the medical model. It also does not purport to deal comprehensively with all mental health impacts of the mill closing. Clearly, the various models of mental health should be applied whenever possible to understand the wide variety of mental health effects. Our effort constitutes but one attempt.

Instrumentation for the Study

Special instrumentation was designed to measure mental health in ways consistent with our model. The psychological impact of the steel mill closings on respondents in the study was measured using indices of alcohol abuse, drug abuse, victimization, apprehensive avoidance, stunned immobility, aggression, acute dependency, helplessness, family relations, anxiety, trust, and hypochondriasis.[9] These indices were constructed from 130 separate agree/disagree items. Each index used six or more items; for example "I am bothered by pains over my heart or in my chest." Both "positively" and "negatively" worded items were included. For postively worded items, *agreement* was coded as 1. For negatively worded items, *disagreement* was coded as a 1. All other responses were coded as 0. Indices were constructed by summing responses to each item. Possible scores ranged from 0 to the total number of items in the index.

The format of the questionnaire and the administration procedure were similar to standard personality inventory instruments such as MMPI.

SCALE ANALYSES

Correlation Analysis

The first step of the analysis was to determine the extent to which the scale responses were intercorrelated. Results of the analysis, in Table 3.8, showed that approximately one-third of the correlation coefficients had moderately high values. Most of the lower valued coefficients were observed when drug abuse and family relations scales were correlated with almost any other scale.

Dimensional Analyses

Since the scales were highly intercorrelated, we performed a dimensional analysis as did Kornhauser (1965, pp. 27-28) in his study of autoworkers. This factor analysis was conducted to scrutinize the patterns of relationships or structures that were associated with the mental health scales.[10] It can be seen in Table 3.9 that three factors account for the underlying structure of the twelve mental health scales. The predominant factor includes nine of the mental health scales. This factor is labeled *stunned immobility*. The factor appears to be tapping emotional helplessness because of the interrelationship of the depression/helplessness, depression immobile, acute depend-

Table 3.8 Pearson's Product-Moment Correlation Coefficients for Paired Comparisons of Mental Health Scales for First-Wave Steelworker Interviews[a]

	Alcohol Abuse	Drug Abuse	Poor Hypo-chondriasis	Victimi-zation	Appre-hensive Avoidance	Depression Immobility	Aggression/ Irritability	Acute Dependency	Depression/ Helplessness	Poor Family Relations	High Anxiety	Lack of Trust/ Suspicious
Alcohol Abuse	—	.17	.35[b]	.41[b]	.20[b]	.44[b]	.40[b]	.36[b]	.37[b]	.41[b]	.45[b]	.41[b]
Drug Abuse		—	.34[b]	.09	.12	.15	.20[b]	.04	.11	.07	.26[b]	.13
Poor Hypochondriasis			—	.38[b]	.25[b]	.47[b]	.33[b]	.38[b]	.30[b]	.12	.58[b]	.43[b]
Victimization				—	.44[b]	.62[b]	.49[b]	.61[b]	.70[b]	.34[b]	.51[b]	.70[b]
Apprehensive Avoidance					—	.51[b]	.42[b]	.42[b]	.46[b]	.14	.38[b]	.47[b]
Depression Immobile						—	.56[b]	.53[b]	.70[b]	.27[b]	.59[b]	.55[b]
Aggression/Irritability							—	.52[b]	.52[b]	-.28[b]	.61[b]	.53[b]
Acute Dependency								—	.64[b]	.29[b]	.56[b]	.68[b]
Depression/Helplessness									—	.34[b]	.60[b]	.64[b]
Poor Family Relations										—	.19[b]	.41[b]
High Anxiety											—	.61[b]
Lack of Trust/Suspicious												—

a. Number of respondents equal 266.
b. Indicates significance at $p < .05$.

Table 3.9   Results of a Factor Analysis of First-Wave Steelworker
Mental Health Scale Scores

Mental Health Scale	Factors			Commonality (h^2)
	I Stunned Immobility	II Poor Hypo-chondriasis	III Trust (spurious)	
Depression/Helplessness	.807	.108	.177	.695
Victimization	.804	.133	.063	.669
Acute Dependency	.752	.157	.057	.593
Depression Immobile	.685	.282	.268	.621
Aggression/Irritability	.571	.289	.336	.523
High Anxiety	.554	.534	.377	.735
Poor Family Relations	.443	.077	.129	.219
Apprehensive Avoidance	.507	.133	.185	.309
Alcohol Abuse	.457	.314	.047	.310
Hypochondriasis	.311	.617	.171	.508
Drug Abuse	.034	.564	.122	.334
Lack of Trust/Suspicious	.032	.026	.631	.401
Eigenvalues	5.34	.70	.59	
Percentage Total Variance	41.1	5.4	4.5	
Percentage Common Variance	80.6	10.5	8.9	

ency, and victimization scales. Also contained in the factor are anxiety, agression/irritability, and alcohol consumption.

A second factor might be labeled *hypochondriasis,* since it loaded primarily on this scale. One interpretation of the factor is that individuals may exhibit emotional maladjustment to personal crisis by converting emotional problems into vague body (somatic) complaints that he or she is attempting to alleviate with medication (most likely over-the-counter drugs). These emotional problems may be associated with high anxiety.

A third factor derived from the lack of trust/suspicious scale. Given the absence of other high loadings, the factor appears to be spurious.[11]

Table 3.10   Reliability Coefficients for Steelworkers'
Wave 1 Sample

Mental Health Scale	Cronbach's Alpha	Standard Cronbach's Alpha*
Alcohol Abuse	.79	.80
Drug Abuse	.27	.00
Hypochondriasis	.60	.62
Victimization	.63	.66
Apprehensive Avoidance	.63	.70
Depression Immobile	.61	.64
Aggression/Irritability	.73	.73
Acute Dependency	.63	.66
Depression/Helplessness	.73	.76
Poor Family Relations	.06	.33
High Anxiety	.59	.60
Lack of Trust/Suspicious	.57	.62

*Computed by dividing alpha by standard deviation.

Reliability

Several reliability tests were conducted on the twelve mental health scales for first- and second-wave data.

Results for steelworkers on the first wave in Table 3.10 show that overall the mental health scales are acceptable for present purposes.[12] Similar findings were obtained when analyzing the scale scores for other groups in the study.

Validity

For purposes of this analysis, *validity* was defined generally as "the extent to which scientifically valuable or practically useful inferences can be drawn from" test scores (Jensen, 1980, p. 297).

Content validity. A test is said to have *content* validity "to the extent that the items in the test are judged to constitute a representative sample of some clearly specified universe of knowledge" (p. 297), such as the mental health of a respondent. "The judgment is usually based on a consensus of experts in the field of knowledge" (p. 297).

In this study, three mental health experts with different psychology backgrounds independently examined the test instrument.[13] All agreed that the test instrument *did* measure mental health from the perspective adopted in this study.

Next, the three experts were shown a random sample of respondent test results. They were asked to evaluate the results and separate the respondents into three categories: those with severe mental health problems, those showing symptoms of stress, and those who appeared to be normal. The three experts agreed on 96 percent of the cases classified.

Both tests of validity enhanced our confidence that we were in fact measuring mental health of respondents from a social-psychological perspective.

Concurrent validity. Concurrent validity may be defined as "the correlation between a new, unvalidated test and another test of already established validity" (Jensen, 1980, p. 300). In this study, one effort at establishing concurrent validity was undertaken.

One indicator of an individual's physical health would be his or her self-evaluation. Respondents were asked, "How would you rate your (physical) health at present? Excellent, good, fair, or poor." Responses to this question were correlated with the physical health scale from the mental health test instrument. Results of the analysis showed that self-evaluations of physical health were correlated ($r = .24$, $p < .001$) with the physical health scale.

CONCLUSION

Plant closings are extraordinarily complex socioeconomic events. They affect thousands of people in disparate ways over a period of years. Individuals and families affected may respond to the event in unique fashion, sometimes successfully, other times disastrously.

Some of the major public policy concerns regarding impacts and coping responses in this study focused on differences between the following groups: workers who are employed, jobless, rehired, or retired; workers in management and those in blue-collar occupations; husbands, wives, and children; workers who are nonminorities and minorities; older and younger workers; and workers with different levels of education. Since these groups may experience different levels of impact and employ different kinds of responses in coping as time passes, this study looked closely at groups one and two years following the closing. A study of minority workers was also conducted four years after the closing.

The complexity of plant closings renders analysis of their effects the subject of multidisciplinary inquiry. As a result, researchers are forced to make difficult choices concerning which methodologies to select in order to guide the study. In this study, we have chosen a social-psychological model of mental health. This model, unlike those found in medically oriented research, tends to emphasize the positive aspects of mental health.

Using the social-psychological model offered us more opportunities to construct our own instrumentation to assess the psychological impact of the mill closing. In the process we sacrificed our ability to compare results from our study with norms established for other populations. Rather than generalize our findings to other populations, we have chosen to conduct within-group analyses to determine relative differences among our subsamples.

We have also chosen to use survey research as a means of gathering data, rather than clinical psychological techniques. Here, we were able to contact a much larger number of people at the expense of producing detailed, highly personalized data about individuals. In this way, we are better able to make statistical inferences about our population.

Since survey research tends to be insensitive to details about individuals when it concerns large samples of people, we also included in our study several case studies of steelworker families affected by the closings. These give some substance to the more general survey results in the study.

Chapter 4 provides an overview of the survey research findings of our study. Chapter 5 follows with individual case studies illustrating the varieties of impact and coping behavior experienced by workers in the study.

Notes

1. Unfortunately, children were not included because of the high cost involved in locating them during the summer months.

2. Workers were from U.S. Steel and Republic Steel. Both facilities are located near the shutdown Campbell and Brier Hill works of Youngstown Sheet and Tube.

3. Our findings are consistent with data developed by the Ohio Bureau of Employment Services for the Youngstown area (see also Bagshaw & Schnorbus, 1980).

4. It was impossible to make inferences about minorities among white-collar workers, since so few minorities hold white-collar positions in the steel industry.

5. Because of space limitations, data were not reported in the text.

6. See note 5.

7. Age and education for spouses of steelworkers and managers were also analyzed. Results of this analysis showed that spouses were slightly younger and less educated than their partners.

8. Prior approval to conduct the study and a public endorsement were secured from the six local United Steelworker Unions representing the Youngstown area. Mass media coverage was also secured to foster a high level of awareness that the study was being conducted in the community. Appropriate law enforcement and human service agency officials were also notified. Next, a questionnaire was designed by a carefully selected staff of ten experts with credentials in psychology, mental health, sociology, and human services. The questionnaire was then pretested on a random sample of thirty steelworkers from the Youngstown area. A list of employees at Youngstown Sheet and Tube was secured. A random sample of steelworkers and managers was drawn. Respondents in the sample were sent a letter-of-intent by the authors explaining the purpose of the study and requesting permission to conduct an interview. The letters-of-intent were then followed by a telephone call from an interviewer to set up a time and place for the interview. In nearly every case, interviews were conducted at the home of the respondent. Staff workers conducted interviews separately with each member of a family. Workers, spouses, and children were not permitted to hear the responses of any other family member in the study. In some cases, interviewers returned on different occasions to complete interviews with family members who were not home during the initial interview. Interviews were highly structured and consisted of closed- and open-ended responses read to respondents by the interviewer. Questions

pertaining to mental health indicators were completed by respondents in a self-administered paper-and-pencil format. Respondents were permitted to seal their reponses in a special envelope, so that the interviewer could not see them at any time. None chose to do this. Interviews required about 150 minutes to complete. Some 700 different observations were collected for each respondent. Interviewers were experienced, well-trained staff members of the Center for Urban Studies at Youngstown State University. Interviewers received some eight hours of training. Only those with an aptitude for interviewing in this context were retained on the project. To insure honesty, approximately twenty percent of the completed interviews were verified by management staff at the center. At the completion of the interview, respondents were informed that they would be contacted in the future, possibly for another interview.

9. Instrumentation was prepared by David Cliness. Because of space limitations, items composing each scale were omitted from the text. Information on scale construction is available from the authors.

10. Group scale scores for first and second wave interviews were factor analyzed independently (separately). Principal axis solution with R^2 as the initial estimate of h^2 loadings was rotated by varimax criteria to simple structure. Table 3.9 displays the results for factors with eigenvalues above 1.0 for steelworkers on the first wave.

11. Rather than exclude this factor in the rotational procedure, we decided to include it in order for it to absorb all of the variance it could, so that the first two factors could be more easily extracted. Similar analyses were performed on mental health scores for managers, spouses, and children. Results, although not identical, were similar enough to suggest that our instrumentation was measuring common factors for each group.

12. Cronbach's alpha computes maximum likelihood estimates of the reliability coefficient when a parallel model is assumed, juxtaposed against the standardized alpha, which corrects Cronbach's alpha by dividing it by the standard deviation of the scale; it was apparent that little increase in magnitude between the alpha and standardized alpha was observed. This suggested that the standard deviations of the scales could not have overly inflated or deflated the alpha coefficient, and that alpha probably represents an acceptable estimate of the reliability of the scales.

13. Two experts had clinicial and psychometric backgrounds. The other was a psychotherapist in a mental health clinic. All had at least ten years of experience.

Chapter 4

PSYCHOLOGICAL IMPACT
OF A PLANT CLOSING

The Youngstown Sheet and Tube Campbell Works closing announcement occurred in September 1977. Over the following six months, over 4,000 workers were permanently let go or forced to accept early retirement. Small portions of the mills remained active and there were occasional recalls; however, most of those terminated during this period would never again work for Sheet and Tube or its successor, Jones & Laughlin.

This chapter focuses on the psychological stresses experienced by these workers and their families in the two years following the closing. A demographic profile of the terminated steelworkers is given in Chapter 3. These effects are measured in the aggregate using the mental health scales described in the preceding chapter. The panel design and comparison groups of employed workers allow the following comparisons of:

- managers and wage workers;
- husbands and spouses;
- blacks, whites, and other ethnic minorities (foreign-born or with English as a second language);
- differences in impact one year and two years after the closing;

- differences in impact related to whether workers were unemployed when interviewed, had been rehired into new jobs, were retired, or had been continuously employed over the two-year period.

The emphasis of this analysis is on intergroup comparisons. The methodology is not intended to measure precisely the rate of incidence of various stress reactions or of mental disorder. Nevertheless, we can determine roughly the proportions of workers reporting severe emotional or behavioral problems and, by comparison with still-employed workers, roughly the level of effects attributable to job loss and/or unemployment.

HYPOTHESES

The literature on psychological impacts of job loss suggests several hypotheses:

(1) Coping behavior for all groups is likely to become *more* effective as time passes, with perhaps two exceptions:

(a)   those who remain unemployed for long periods of time will be *less* effective in coping than others, and

(b)   those who are laid off more than once will be *less* effective in coping than others.

Human beings are extraordinarily resilient when it comes to coping with personal disaster. It is always surprising to see how much adversity individuals can tolerate. Therefore, our expectation is that laid-off workers, although severely affected in the short term, will eventually make a comeback. Succumbing to stressful events is simply not tolerated by most people over the long run.

Obviously, the most important factor assisting workers in coping is the resumption of secure employment. All the better if this employment is equivalent or more desirable than that which was lost.

(2) Those who remain unemployed, either white- or blue-collar workers, will be *less* effective in coping and more likely to experience emotional distress than others who retire involuntarily or quickly find new jobs.

The extent to which job loss implies a loss of financial security, sense of degradation, and uncertainty depends on what follows. Retirement, especially early or unanticipated retirement, where financial resources are likely to be meager or preparation for retirement is likely to be insufficient, may be as stressful as unemployment. However, those who quickly find new employment will experience least stress.

(3) White-collar workers will cope *more* effectively with job loss than will blue-collar workers.

White-collar workers are typically more mobile than their blue-collar counterparts. White-collar workers may have job skills that are in demand in a wider variety of industries than for blue-collar workers. An accountant, for example, might be able to work in any industry, while a blast furnace worker might not. White-collar workers also may have better job search skills. White-collar workers are more educated, often communicate better orally and in writing, are more well versed in resume preparation, and are more adept at the job interview. White-collar workers are also much less reluctant to migrate in search of jobs than are blue-collar workers. As a result of this apparent mobility, white-collar workers should be less affected by or less apprehensive about a plant closing than other workers.

(4) Regardless of occupational status, the *more* problems in coping that are experienced, the *less* effective will be the coping behaviors of the worker's family.

The stress of job loss or potential job loss experienced by workers is likely to induce stress reactions among family members. The ways in which this might be manifested are legion, but some examples might suffice. A husband who has lost his job may be forced to relinquish his role as breadwinner to his wife, who may have or may find a job. A worker's self-esteem, pride, and sense of worth may be lost, creating stress on family relationships and perhaps ultimately leading to divorce. A worker may attempt to reduce stress by consuming too much alcohol. This may cause the worker to take out his frustration on his family, abusing his children or wife. A child of a laid-off worker may be informed that financial resources for attending college are no longer available. The child, unable to cope with this disastrous change in plans, may become delinquent, dropping out of high school. Not all stress due to job loss is likely to be so severe as the examples just presented. But it is likely that stress will dramatically lower the quality of family life by weakening positive family relationships or exacerbating existing negative ones.

(5) Families of white-collar workers will be *more* effective in coping than families of blue-collar workers.

As implied above, a lack of mobility to secure employment can be devastating once job loss occurs. White-collar workers, having far greater mobility, are less likely to be damaged by job loss. As a result, their families may not be as likely to be subjected to stress-producing situations.

(6) Minority workers will be *less* successful in coping with job loss than nonminorities.

Minority workers probably confront more severe personal problems when their jobs are terminated. Minority workers who lack seniority will often be the first fired and the last rehired. In addition, outright or subtle job discrimination may make it more difficult for minorities to find replacement jobs for those lost.

In the sections below, these hypotheses will be tested statistically based on data from the Youngstown studies.

EMPLOYMENT STATUS AND MENTAL HEALTH

Several patterns of change in employment status were possible for both terminated and nonterminated workers. Workers left for new jobs, some were laid off for short periods of time and brought back, others took early retirement, and some remained continuously employed. Analysis began by examining steelworker mental health scores on the first and second waves as shown in Table 4.1.

On each scale, the unemployed showed more stress symptoms than those who had found new jobs, were retired, or were continuously employed. Although these results are consistent with expectations about unemployment—not having a job is more stressful than having one—only four of the scale differences were statistically significant. The unemployed were likely to consume more alcohol and to experience family problems. These findings are consistent with other studies that link short-term increased alcohol consumption to job loss as a common coping behavior among the unemployed (see Weeks & Drengacz, 1982; Sadava, Thistle, & Forsyth, 1978). Other findings have linked job loss to such things as child abuse and marital problems (see Steinberg, Catalano, & Dooley, 1981). The unemployed also felt more victimized and anxious than others. By the second wave, all significant differences had disappeared. However, the direction of differences suggest still that the unemployed were worse off on each scale than was the case for the other groups.

First-wave patterns for the unemployed are repeated on the second wave. The unemployed have more family problems than the retired or rehired. Surprisingly, the same is true for the continuously employed, which served as a comparison group. Rehired workers exhibit the lowest level of feelings of helplessness and unemployed workers are the most depressed of the four groups, while retired workers are significantly less depressed than all others.

Table 4.1   First Wave[a] Mean Scores for Steelworkers'
             Mental Health Scales

Mental Health Scale	Steelworkers[d]				Total Mean Score	Statistical Significance
	Unemployed	Retired	Rehired[b]	Employed[c]		
Health Problems	.24	−.12	−.09	−.05	4.15	.310
Alcohol Consumption	.38	−.13	−.10	−.10	.39	.013[e]
Drug Usage	.03	−.11	−.08	−.02	.96	.426
Family Problems	.22	−.35	.05	−.04	2.04	.017[e]
Aggression	.66	−.58	−.10	−.14	1.88	.090
Anxiety	.62	−.59	−.03	−.12	1.69	.012[e]
Avoidance	.36	.04	−.19	−.10	1.84	.355
Depressed	.23	−.42	−.11	.02	1.03	.218
Helplessness	.38	−.55	−.01	−.05	1.03	.144
Lacks Trust	.46	−.38	−.04	−.00	1.71	.102
Victimized	.57	−.43	−.49	.02	1.20	.001[e]
Acute Dependency	.32	−.09	−.42	.03	2.33	.273

a. To simplify this table and because no significant differences were observed for the second wave, second wave scores have been omitted.
b. Rehired other than at Sheet and Tube.
c. Currently employed at Sheet and Tube.
d. Figures are mean deviations.
e. Indicates statistical significance at $p < .05$.

The small sample sizes and the minimal differences found preclude any firm conclusions with regard to group differences in emotional problems. The consistency of our findings overall, however, leads us to believe that although being laid off is a stressful life event, it may not, in many cases, produce severe mental disorders in those affected. In short, unemployed workers may exhibit levels of mild depression similar to those who have retired or are employed.

Additionally, the Youngstown findings suggest that effects of job loss are related to continuing unemployment rather than the initial shock of job loss. Such a conclusion is consistent with Cobb and Kasl's (1977, p. 175) finding that terminated workers "with more unemployment did respond with strikingly, and very significantly, more anxiety and tension than those with less."

It appears that those forced to retire early were not subject to amounts of stress sufficient to produce psychological problems. Indeed, retired workers may have felt relief in finally terminating a career that was for many dirty, noisy, and extremely dangerous (see Terkel, 1974). The fact that retirement benefits were, for many, sufficient to maintain accustomed lifestyles may also have been a factor.

In Chapter 3, it was observed that many workers were laid off, rehired, laid off again, only to be rehired again. It appeared that sporadic unemployment was less damaging than might be expected. Although not conclusively demonstrated, it appears that brief periods of unemployment may have allowed a worker and his family to grow accustomed to the reality of a plant shutdown, perhaps in much the same way as periodic layoffs in the steel industry tend to inoculate workers against the deleterious effects of unemployment. Another view might be that social support networks mitigate the stress of short-term job loss (e.g., Gore, 1978). Over the long term, however, financial hardship, social isolation, decline in quality of life, decreased life chances or opportunities, and so on may eventually erode stress suppressors, so that more severe depression would begin to appear (e.g., Rueth & Heller, 1981).

Somewhat less straightforward explanations may be required to account for the findings concerning the continuously employed. Those who were continuously employed exhibited stress sometimes as debilitating as those who had lost their jobs. This may have occurred because employed workers were continually exposed to conflicting reports and rumors about impending further job retrenchment or shutdowns. This information appeared to run rampant through the workers' rumor mills, union organizations, and in the local mass media. Workers were quite unsure from day to day how they might be affected. Consequently, workers may have been unable to effectively plan rational actions in anticipation of further events.[1]

WHITE- VERSUS BLUE-COLLAR

Table 4.2 shows comparisons for managers and steelworkers on the first (summer 1978) and second (summer 1979) waves of the study for thirteen mental health scales. Manager and steelworker scores differed significantly on seven of the thirteen scales under analysis. All seven comparisons showed that managers were less affected one year after the closing than were steelworkers. Steelworkers, relative to managers, felt more helpless, victimized, and distrustful. They tended to avoid social interaction and were more aggressive. In addition, they were more depressed and exhibited a greater degree of perceived immobility. Other analyses suggested that these group differences were primarily accounted for by the depression and immobility scales. Apparently, the seven-group differences above are measuring différent appearances of depression[2] accompanied by a lack of mobility.

Changes in steelworker and manager scores were also analyzed for one- and two-year periods following the closing. Steelworkers were less trustful than they were on the first wave and they continued to exhibit signs of immobility, helplessness and, anxiety. Importantly, steelworkers reported having increased their consumption of alcohol and were experiencing more health problems. Ironically, family problems were reported to have abated somewhat.

Managers, by contrast, were coping much better than steelworkers. With the exception of an increase in lack of trust, managers continued to improve or remained unchanged on the scales under analysis.

Managers and steelworkers differed in their responses on several scales on the second wave. In general, steelworkers were more severely affected by the closing than managers. Steelworkers were more aggressive and anxious. Steelworkers reported a greater sense of victimization, distrust, and helplessness. They were more depressed and experienced more somatic problems. Alcohol consumption was greater than for

Table 4.2   Mental Health Scale Comparisons (Mean Scores)
for Steelworkers Versus Managers Assessed on
the First and Second Waves

Scale	First Wave Second Wave	Steelworkers	Manager	Z-Score
Physical Weakness		.60 .43	.50 .11	.64 1.61
Health Problems		4.15 5.49	4.05 2.11	.40 13.08[a]
Alcohol Consumption		.39 1.45	.29 .07	.67 8.98[a]
Drug Usage		.96 .69	.94 .93	.90 2.20[a]
Family Problems		2.04 .83	1.86 1.93	1.50 4.35[a]
Aggression		1.88 1.47	1.25 .32	2.16[a] 3.58[a]
Anxiety		1.69 1.39	1.26 1.07	1.94 4.51[a]
Avoidance		1.84 1.56	1.24 .82	2.22[a] 3.06[a]
Immobility		1.03 1.37	.49 .17	3.00[a] 1.17
Helplessness		1.03 1.09	.53 .18	2.28[a] 3.54[a]
Lacks Trust		1.71 3.33	1.09 1.64	2.75[a] 6.98[a]
Victimized		1.20 1.14	.67 .58	2.44[a] 2.01[a]
Depressed		2.33 1.75	1.55 1.23	3.10[a] 1.60[a]
Sample Size		245 140	51 28	

a. Indicates statistical significance at $p < .05$.

mangers. Managers reported more family problems than had steelworkers. Unlike steelworkers, they were more likely to use over-the-counter drugs.

Overall, our findings suggested that managers and steelworkers were both suffering from relatively mild depression induced as a result of stress due to employment circumstances. Depression, as observed in other studies, was found to manifest itself in a variety of ways. Managers were more effective at coping with stress initially and over the longer term than were steelworkers. One explanation for this may be that managers had more resources and more positive options, whereas steelworkers perceived themselves as highly constrained in their choice of alternatives.

Variations in coping behavior also may have resulted from social class or status differences between managers and steelworkers. Managers, for example, coped with depression to some extent by *self-medication* by means of over-the-counter drugs (e.g., aspirin and sleeping pills). Steelworkers, by contrast, self-medicated with increased alcohol consumption. This is, of course, highly speculative and should not be over-interpreted (see Levitt & Lubin, 1976).

Steelworkers seemed to have more somatic problems than managers. One interpretation of this finding is that steelworkers may be masking depression (Kielholz, 1973), which in turn has led to or been manifested as physical health problems. This would be consistent with many other findings (Sheppard et al., 1966; Tessler, Mechanic, & Dimond, 1976; Dohrenwend & Dohrenwend, 1974).

ETHNIC AND RACIAL DIFFERENCES

Mental health effects due to job loss were also investigated for workers classified by ethnicity and race. As noted in the previous chapter, minorities were classified as European ethnics (including eastern and southern European and Spanish-speaking minorities) and blacks. All others were designated as nonminorities.

Before considering the results of these analysis, it should be noted that previous studies have shown that there are significant racial and/or ethnic differences in personality assessment scores, regardless of the external stimulus of such events as a plant closing. It is known, for example, that there are different value systems, perceptions and expectations among different groups and that these differences are reflected in assessment scores (see Cross, Barclay, & Barger, 1978; Gynther, 1972; Waldron, Kerchauf, & Sutton, 1981). These studies suggest that any statistical differences obtained should not be considered as necessarily indicating more or less pathology in one or another group.

Table 4.3 shows mental health scores for minorities on three waves of the study—summer 1978, 1979, and 1981—as well as scores for nonminorities on two waves—summer 1978 and 1979.

Results in Table 4.3 show both persistence and change across the mental health indicators examined. Nonminorities, relative to other groups, exhibited fewer feelings of weakness, victimization, helplessness, and depression on both the first and second waves. Nonminorities tended to experience fewer somatic problems than blacks, but not European ethnics, on the first wave; and fewer somatic problems than either blacks or European ethnics on the second.

Two years after the second wave interviews, blacks were more likely than European ethnic minorities to exhibit family problems and a sense of victimization. European ethnic minorities were less likely than blacks to experience somatic problems.[3]

Next, analysis examined the trends in mental health scores for black and European ethnic minorities over the three time periods. Remarkably, scores for both groups manifested statistically significant identical trends with but one exception: blacks appeared to become somewhat less depressed between the first and second waves, but more depressed by the third wave. Ethnic minorities behaved just the opposite. None of the statistically significant patterns of change showed blacks and

Table 4.3 Mental Health Scale Comparisons (Mean Scores) for Minority and Nonminority Steelworkers[a]

Scale	First Wave (Summer 1978)			Second Wave (Summer 1979)			Third Wave (Summer 1981)		
	Nonminority	Minority		Nonminority	Minority		Nonminority	Minority	
		Black	Ethnic		Black	Ethnic		Black	Ethnic
Physical Weakness	.55[b]	.96	.47	.27[b]	.75	.71	x[b]	.89	.72
Health Problems	4.09[b]	4.55	3.66	4.72[b]	5.97	5.11	x	4.20[b]	3.70
Alcohol Consumption	.35	.46	.47	1.12[b]	1.39	1.75	x	1.01	1.11
Drug Usage	.95	.97	1.11	.69[b]	.69	1.00	x	1.00	.93
Family Problems	2.03	1.89	2.17	.97	1.15	1.10	x	2.28[b]	1.69
Aggression	1.81	1.55	1.69	1.18	1.70	1.65	x	1.38	1.71
Anxiety	1.65	1.57	1.27	2.11	2.55	2.48	x	1.75	2.05
Avoidance	1.68	1.91	2.14	1.38	1.55	1.97	x	1.89	1.53
Immobility	.96[b]	.74	1.40	1.02[b]	1.81	1.48	x	1.15	1.09
Helplessness	.95[b]	.83	1.28	.83[b]	1.27	1.47	x	1.16	1.39
Lacks Trust	1.57	1.80	1.76	2.94[b]	3.81	3.79	x	2.70	2.40
Victimized	1.06[b]	1.40	1.17	.86[b]	1.77	1.37	x	2.81[b]	2.24
Depressed	2.11[b]	2.60	2.47	1.58[b]	1.69	2.56	x	2.29	2.38
Sample Size									

a. Nonminorities were not interviewed in the third wave (see Chapter 3).
b. Indicates statistical significance at $p < .05$.

European ethnic minorities consistently coping better from the first wave to the second and from the second wave to the third.

Victimization was the only mental health indicator that appeared to become worse over the four-year period for blacks and ethnic minorities. Minorities improved their psychological well-being on at least four scales. From the first to the second wave, minorities tended to feel more anxious and distrustful. This was accompanied by an increased sense of immobility. Alcohol consumption also was reported to have increased. Somatic problems were reported to have abated. By the third wave, all of these dysfunctional trends began to abate.

Minorities appeared to be improving on family problems, only to become worse three years later. One interpretation of this trend is that minorities initially felt immobilized by job loss. Lack of perceived mobility may have been associated with increased feelings of anxiety about prospects for the future. Distrust of others and a sense of victimization accompanied these feelings. Those affected tended to medicate themselves by means of alcoholic beverage consumption. Families may have pulled together during this period as evidenced by a decrease in family-related problems.

Two years later, minorities were beginning to rid themselves of many psychological problems. The members of the family, apparently unable to withstand increased stress, seemed to have experienced increased strain on relationships. A sense of victimization continued to persist among minorities through this period.

It appears that psychological problems manifested in a variety of ways; many continue to plague minorities at least four years following a closing. Much of this might be explained by job discrimination practices. Laid-off minorities may be among the last to find jobs and may find their new jobs to be less satisfactory or stable. As a result, the burdens of unemployment may be compounded by discrimination.

FAMILIES

Managers versus steelworkers. Because of the near absence of females in many steel industry occupations, the Youngstown worker samples only include males. Table 4.4 compares mental health scale scores for steelworker's and manager's wives on the first and second waves.

When first interviewed, steelworker and manager spouses differed significantly on only two scales. As was the case with their husbands, steelworker wives were less likely to medicate themselves with over-the-counter drugs than were manager wives. By contrast, steelworker wives were more likely to express and report aggression than their manager counterparts.

Wives, regardless of their husband's occupational status, appeared to be coping better since nearly all of the scale scores for both groups decreased or remained stable from the first to the second wave. Two important exceptions were for steelworker wives. They tended to report increased somatic problems and increased use of alcohol.

By the second wave, more significant differences were observed. Steelworker wives exhibited more aggression, anxiety, helplessness, distrust, and avoidance than manager wives. Steelworker wives reported increased use of alcohol and more somatic problems than manager's wives. Again, as was the case for their husbands, significant differences were accounted for by depression and immobility.

Generally, these findings parallel those for steelworkers and managers. Wives in both groups were suffering from mild depression as a result of stress from their husband's loss of work. Wives of managers were somewhat less affected by the closing than wives of steelworkers. Both groups effectively coped with the crisis by the second year.

The use of drugs by manager wives and alcohol by steelworker wives again seemed to reinforce the notion that social class or status was in part a determinant in the coping process of individuals. Importantly, steelworker wives likes their husbands may have been masking depression which became manifested as somatic problems (Kielholz, 1973). These problems were alleviated by increased alcohol consumption. By

Table 4.4   Mental Health Scale Comparisons (Mean Scores)
for Steelworker's and Manager's Wives on the
First and Second Waves

Scale *First Wave* *Second Wave*	Spouses		
	Steelworker	*Manager*	*Z-Score*
Physical Weakness	.84	.68	.62
	.35	.22	.77
Health Problems	3.00	2.85	1.20
	5.66	2.71	9.95^a
Alcohol Consumption	.13	.00	1.40
	1.28	.04	7.09^a
Drug Usage	.99	1.18	2.32^a
	.75	1.05	2.51^a
Family Problems	2.15	2.17	.39
	.91	1.81	3.78^a
Aggression	1.78	1.09	2.10^a
	1.12	.85	1.01^a
Anxiety	1.64	1.44	.63
	1.42	.87	2.04^a
Avoidance	1.59	1.29	.89
	1.42	.87	2.04^a
Immobility	.86	.66	.89
	.98	.26	2.68^a
Helplessness	1.07	.76	1.10
	.86	.45	1.96^a
Lacks Trust	1.35	1.24	.44
	2.48	.79	3.74^a
Victimized	.94	.76	.78
	.68	.48	1.08
Depressed	2.19	2.08	.97
	1.16	1.95	2.92^a
Sample Size	197	38	
	125	26	

a. Indicates statistical significance at $p < .05$.

contrast, manager wives were mildly depressed and may have treated themselves with aspirin or sleeping pills.

Husbands and wives. Next, group mental health scores for steelworkers and managers were matched with those for wives, respectively. Both sets of group comparisons showed few significant differences between husbands and wives. Only one significant difference was observed on the first wave: Husbands, both steelworkers and managers, were more likely to report somatic problems than were their spouses. By the second wave, these differences had diminished.

On the second wave, several differences were observed. Steelworkers were more likely to feel immobilized than their wives. No differences were observed between managers and their wives. Again, the depression scale emerged as important: Steelworkers were more depressed than their wives, but among the managerial group, the converse of this was the case.

In an analysis reported elsewhere (see Buss & Redburn, 1983a), individual scores were compared for steelworkers and their wives. Results showed that the scores of husbands were largely unrelated to those of their wives. Apparently, stress in one partner is not necessarily transferred to the other partner.

Wives and employment status. We then considered the effect of employment status of the husband on the mental health of the wife. Initial expectations were that the stress experienced by unemployed workers would be transferred to their wives. Results of this analysis are presented in Table 4.5.

Surprisingly, the expected transfer of problems from husband to spouse as a result of unemployment was not widely observed. This was the case in both the first and second waves.[4] Spouses of workers who were unemployed reported feeling more aggressive, helpless, and victimized than other wives whose husbands were employed or retired.

Children

If job loss places stress on families and changes long-term financial and employment prospects for breadwinners, these

Table 4.5   Mental Health Scale Comparisons (Mean Scores) for Spouses (Managers and Steelworkers)[a] on the Second Wave[b]

	Unemployed	Retired	Rehired	Employed	F
Physical Weakness	.34	.09	.38	.32	.39
Health Problems	4.79	4.13	4.42	4.43	.34
Alcohol Consumption	1.38	1.01	1.19	1.38	.51
Drug Usage	.79	.78	.69	.71	.12
Family Problems	1.47	.26	.81	.93	1.96
Aggression	2.01	.76	1.39	.97	2.63[c]
Anxiety	2.77	1.63	2.08	2.20	1.59
Avoidance	1.97	1.04	1.23	1.46	1.49
Immobility	1.52	.60	.85	1.00	.98
Helplessness	1.73	.22	.88	.82	5.33[c]
Lacks Trust	1.65	2.02	2.66	2.68	.74
Victimized	1.43	.29	.81	.59	3.53[c]
Depressed	1.94	1.29	1.15	1.04	1.79
Sample Size	13	8	26	55	

a. Because of the small subsamples for those who were not in the employed group, manager and steelworker spouse data was merged.
b. First wave results omitted from tabular presentation because of spatial considerations.
c. Indicates statistical significance at $p < .05$.

changes may affect children (e.g., Steinberg et al., 1981). Two separate studies were conducted to determine the psychological impact of the steel mill closing on children (see Chapter 3 for a description of these studies). The first involved an analysis of children of workers who were interviewed in this study on the first wave. The second focused on a group of college students whose parent(s) was laid off from Sheet and Tube and who subsequently received special scholarships to attend Youngstown State University. Table 4.6 shows the results of the first study.

Table 4.6 shows that children of steelworkers and managers responded in ways similar to those of their fathers. Steelworker children reported more somatic problems and more family problems than manager children. Steelworker children also felt more immobile, more helpless, and more victimized than manager children.

Table 4.6   Mental Health Scale Comparisons (Mean Scores)
             for Steelworkers' and Managers' Children on the
             First Wave Controlling on Employment Status

| | Father is a | | | Father is | | |
Scale	Manager	Steelworker	F	Employed	Unemployed	F
Physical Weakness	.71	1.07	2.07	.89	1.06	1.51
Health Problems	3.18	3.74	6.57^a	3.46	3.94	1.15
Alcohol Consumption	.29	.16	1.34	.15	.18	1.05
Drug Usage	.76	.85	1.31	.79	.94	1.36
Family Problems	2.06	2.19	3.12^a	2.23	2.10	1.22
Aggression	1.94	3.10	1.52	2.97	2.83	1.07
Anxiety	1.71	2.10	1.76	2.05	1.92	1.04
Avoidance	1.41	1.97	1.12	2.03	1.54	2.17^a
Immobility	.59	1.26	4.56^a	1.11	1.10	1.20
Helplessness	1.18	1.77	2.53^a	3.03	2.23	1.40
Lacks Trust	1.29	1.96	1.23	2.06	1.42	2.02^a
Victimized	.88	1.79	3.55^a	1.67	1.63	1.02
Depressed	2.18	2.85	1.20	3.03	2.23	1.40
Sample Size	17	100		66	48	

a. Indicates statistical significance of $p < .05$.

Results seemed to illustrate that there are differences in blue-collar and white-collar family response to everyday life. Blue-collar workers, again because of the constrictions of immobility, do not cope as effectively as their white-collar counterparts. Apparently, this is passed along to children in the respective families.

Data for children were next analyzed to determine if those whose fathers were employed responded differently than those whose fathers were unemployed. Results, in Table 4.6, show that they responded similarly on our thirteen scales with two exceptions: Children of the unemployed were more likely to avoid social interaction and were more distrustful than children of the employed.

It appears that the employment status of fathers was not a major factor in accounting for coping behaviors exhibited or reported by children. At least one year following the closing, the severe psychological impacts which might be expected were not forthcoming. This may have been the case because many terminated workers either found jobs, expected to find jobs, or were still receiving unemployment benefits. Financial hardships or material deprivation may not have been sufficient at this stage to induce stress in families. This data set does not, however, address the long-term impacts that might occur.

An analysis of college students whose parents were laid off from Youngstown Sheet and Tube does allow us to look more closely at potential longer term impacts. Table 4.7 presents these results in summary form.

There is an absence of significant differences between the students whose fathers had lost their jobs and a comparison group of students who were not affected. When analyzing the data for possible effects concerning differences resulting from the employment status of a parent, a similar absence of significant differences was observed. Although it is not known how these groups might have changed during the four-year period after the closing but prior to this interview, it did appear that there was little evidence of lingering mental health problems among those who might have experienced them.

We attempted to make additional inferences about this group by contacting by telephone the 110 remaining students who were not formally interviewed in our original random sample of 77 college students. Some 64 students were contacted in summer 1981. Data revealed that slightly less than half (N = 26) had left town in search of a better life elsewhere. Nearly one-fifth (N = 13) did not stay in school and obtain their degree; the remaining four-fifths either stayed in school (N = 14) or were able to graduate (N = 37). Interestingly, unemployment did not plague this group as it had their parents; only 5 students were unemployed during the time of the interview.

These findings illustrate a major dilemma faced by distressed communities: Those educational efforts that help young people affected by plant closings and are intended to prepare the next generation of workers to take their place in the community, may eventually give these young people the necessary

Table 4.7   Mental Health Scale Comparisons (Mean Scores) for College Students Whose Parents Were or Were Not Laid Off in the Steel Mill Closings Summer 1981

Scale	Parents Laid Off from Mills	Student Comparison Group	F
Physical Weakness	.43	.49	.147
Health Problems	2.78	2.76	.006
Alcohol Consumption	1.23	1.09	1.034
Drug Usage	.83	.87	.268
Family Problems	2.06	1.96	.606
Aggression	1.64	1.78	.160
Anxiety	1.73	1.75	.004
Avoidance	1.03	1.20	.322
Immobility	.61	.85	1.562
Helplessness	.47	.56	.204
Lacks Trust	1.18	1.20	.006
Victimized	.84	.89	.050
Depressed	2.27	2.44	.223
Sample Size	77	55	

qualifications to move to a better location. This is suggested in part by the low level of unemployment experienced by young people in this group. One consequence of this pattern is that fewer workers will be available to replace those who retire. Distressed communities, then, can expect continuing population declines.

THE IMPACTS OF SUDDEN UNEMPLOYMENT

Summary results for the entire study show that none of the groups was severely affected by the closing, one or two years later. Indeed, psychopathological behavior was no more prevalent among individuals in our samples than one might expect among the general public. Apparently, a vast majority of those who might be presumed to be at risk as a result of the closing were able to cope in positive, functional ways; only a few might be characterized as being severely affected and consequently in need of professional treatment.

What accounts for the relatively mild psychological impact of the closing on these various groups? *First,* nearly 95 percent of the laid-off work force was able to find new jobs or became eligible for retirement (in many cases early retirement) (see Bagshaw & Schnorbus, 1980). This restoration of a modicum of financial security may have reduced stress or depression that might have resulted from immediate loss of income and perhaps the necessity of selling a home, modifying a lifestyle, or migrating to another community. The capacity of a local labor market to absorb those workers who have been laid off may be critically important to either precipitating or lessening potential mental health effects.

Second, steelworkers and managers in the steel industry are among the highest paid workers in the United States. Although they may have had more to lose when a job was terminated, they may have had greater personal resources upon which to draw. In addition, steelworkers, but not managers, received not only unemployment benefits but also supplemental unemployment compensation from their union, as well as additional compensation from the U.S. government. Substantial financial resources of these workers in the short term may have insulated them from more severe psychological impacts. Since not all industries provide high wages and generous benefits, the psychological impacts of a closing may vary depending on the industry.

Third, one reason for high wages paid in the steel industry is that workers are compensated for anticipated, periodic job loss. The steel industry is very much subject to growth and decline fluctuations of national and international economic cycles. During a worker's tenure in the industry, he can expect to be laid off many times only to be called back again. This being the case, workers may over time become inoculated against the short-term effects of unemployment. Those who cannot make this adjustment typically may not pursue occupations in the industry, preferring more stable employment elsewhere. The employment stability of an industry may help explain the extent to which workers are able to cope.

Fourth, Youngstown is a community composed of highly integrated family and social networks. These networks serve a variety of social functions for workers, not the least of which is providing a mechanism for self-help during times of personal or family crisis. These networks may assist in fulfilling the financial needs of workers, may provide therapy for problems, and may be instrumental in locating and obtaining jobs. Of course, those who are not integrated in networks are denied an important helping source in times of crisis (see Rayman, 1982).

Fifth, the use of alcohol or over-the-counter drugs as a means of self-treatment for mild depression may have been quite effective as an antidote against more severe mental and emotional problems. Indeed, the use of substances in the short term and in moderation may be a highly effective coping mechanism for dealing with individual crisis (see Weeks & Drengacz, 1982).

Another coping strategy, which has been observed in other studies of mass unemployment, is participation in group action such as protesting, lobbying, self-help, and so on (Cobb, 1976; Gore, 1978; Dean & Lin, 1977; Lieberman & Boreman, 1976). Getting workers involved is thought to divert their attention away from personal problems by focusing instead on actions that might restore a lost job, secure a new job, or even help another who is less fortunate. In the Youngstown steel mill closings, very little group action was observed (Buss & Hofstetter, 1981). It is unlikely, therefore, that the impacts of the closing were ameliorated to a great extent as a result of group actions.

CONCLUSION

Engel and Schmale (1967) make an important distinction between helplessness and hopelessness: Helplessness is a belief that no one will do anything to help you and hopelessness is a belief that neither you nor anyone else can do anything. These perceived feelings of helplessness, immobility, and depression are central themes in the Sheet and Tube closing. Yet, overall, workers appeared to recover emotionally and to cope fairly successfully with the shock of job loss. Those whose initial coping efforts were less successful experienced the greatest psychological stress. Minority workers were more likely than others to be in this category.

Notes

1, Later events appeared to confirm these fears. In 1979 and 1980, a series of additional mill closings eliminated many of the jobs held by workers in the comparison group.

2. Most researchers distinguish between endogenous and reactive depression. Endogenous forms of this malady are thought to be psychologically based and may have a genetic component. Often this form of depression manifests itself in a psychotic state and an individual is variously affected over long periods of time. Endogenous depression may, at times, be triggered by environmental stimuli, but it is as often a response to internal factors. Obviously, this form of depression is little related to the current study. Reactive depression, as its names implies, is usually the result of pressures from outside the individual. This form of depression is usually, but not always, a neurotic process and manifests itself in several ways. Levitt and Lubin (1975) list 54 symptoms of depression. Psychological symptoms include irritability, crying, guilt, dissatisfaction, helplessness, hopelessness, and feelings of being punished, among others. Seligman (1974) notes that depressive manifestations include (1) passivity, slow response initiation, retardation, and lowered amplitude of behavior; (2) negative expectation (patients construe their acts as failures); and (3) the sense of helplessness, hopelessness, and powerlessness.

3. Nonminority workers were not interviewed on this "third wave."

4. Because of small subsamples when controlling on employment status, it was decided to merge the steelworker and manager subsamples to increase sample sizes. It was, therefore, statistically impossible to analyze potentially important relations concerning employment status and occupation (i.e., blue collar versus management) for our spouse sample.

Chapter 5

PERSONALIZING THE IMPACT
Some Case Studies

It is easy to think about the impact of job loss on workers as though it were a common experience shared by a homogeneous group. However, as with so many other areas of inquiry, useful knowledge begins with differentiation of gross categories and stereotypes. The meaning of job loss to an individual depends greatly on the prior history as well as the present circumstances of that person. These variations can be described in terms of characteristics such as age, family status, financial savings, or access to benefits, education, relationship to network of support (friends, political connections, religious institutions, and so on). Personal variations can simultaneously be defined in psychological terms. Even these categories do not adequately suggest the range and variety of individual and family situations and, therefore, the varied experience that job loss generates.

The case studies reported here help to break down mental stereotypes that stand between us and an adequate understanding of how the meaning of job loss, and its social and psychological effects, vary. The purpose of this chapter is not, therefore, to generalize. This is too small a sampling, in any case, to permit that.[1] Rather, the reported experiences of these workers and their families, in the years since the closing, have given us—and we hope will give readers—an appreciation of how difficult it is to grasp or predict what job loss may mean to individuals. The direct implication is this, also: that policy-makers and human services managers face a complex task when they seek to fashion programs to identify, reach, and help those who are harmed by sudden loss of employment.

Name:	Jon Sherrill
Age:	59
Spouse:	Marianne (deceased); Karen, married 1980
Children:	Two daughters, ages 23 and 24 (both live at home)
Education:	Elementary school
Employment:	Retired March 1978; employed by Youngstown Sheet and Tube Company 1950-1978
Health:	Good, with some respiratory problems
Date laid off:	September 1977
Date recalled:	March 1978 (Chose early retirement rather than take laborer position).

Jon Sherrill, who is black, grew up in the hills of North Carolina. His father worked for over forty years on a railroad wrecking crew but barely earned enough to support his wife and eight children. As a teenager, Jon worked on the railroad as a machinist's helper; but he thought he would never get beyond that position at a time when job opportunities were severely limited in the South.

In 1950, Jon decided to migrate North in search of a better job and higher standard of living. He arrived in Youngstown when the steel mills were hiring many men due to the Korean

War. Jon found work with the Youngstown Sheet and Tube Company as a general laborer and eventually held several other positions including that of ladle pitman. Jon worked in the blast furnaces all day in searing heat and grime. He says the heat did not bother him because, as a child, he suffered long bouts of pleurisy and bronchial pneumonia; the high temperatures helped keep his lungs clear from infection.

Jon's first wife, Marianne, was born and raised in western Pennsylvania. Marianne quit school in the eleventh grade to work and help support her nine brothers and sisters. She arrived in Youngstown about the same time as Jon for a summer visit with relatives and discovered that she liked the city's cleanliness, neat white houses, beautiful parks, and a school system superior to the one which she had attended. Her friends helped her to find work soon as a kitchen helper for an affluent family.

About a year later, Jon and Marianne met through mutual friends and soon married. Jon had a well-paying job as a steel worker. Marianne's small income also contributed to their growing savings. In time, they were able to move from a tiny, cramped apartment in a poorer section of town to a newly built home within walking distance of Mill Creek Park.

Jon, now 59, was one of the first several hundred steel workers to be laid off following the closing announcement. The news was a severe shock to him. He had looked forward to retiring to North Carolina in two years with a substantial pension from nearly thirty years with the mill.

In March 1978, Jon was recalled, but to a general laborer position, which he described as one of the lowest, most ill-paid jobs in the mill. He deeply resented the terms of this offer to return to work and reluctantly decided to retire early under provisions of the "over 65 rule." His retirement benefits were substantially reduced, however. When he retired, he had worked in the mill for 28½ years. He was eligible for Trade Adjustment Allowances (TRA) and Supplemental Union Benefits (SUB).

These benefits helped him to meet expenses for a while, but they expired in October 1978.

In mid-1978, Marianne returned to work as a cook in a federally funded daycare program. She enjoyed cooking, but preferred to stay at home. Her part-time job provided only a meager supplement to the family's income. Marianne began to suffer from painful, crippling headaches that she blamed at least partly on her job. She worked for another few months and quit soon after Christmas 1978.

Jon's eldest daughter, age 23 in 1979, is a line worker at the local automobile assembly plant and lives at home. She earns a very good wage and is self-sufficient. For a while, she paid $100 per month as rent to her parents. Marianne felt the girl should contribute more toward household expenses, while Jon was "too proud" to admit to his daughter that he needed the extra money. The couple argued over this and Marianne even considered asking her daughter to move.

The younger daughter, age 22, is mentally retarded. For some reason, her parents were not informed that their daughter was eligible for special education; consequently, she remained at home, uneducated, for nearly fifteen years. More recently, she has attended a sheltered workshop facility for adults with learning impairments and has made progress. She receives Supplemental Security Income payments that cover the cost of her care.

After retiring, Jon had to make major adjustments in his schedule. When working, he said he had little time or energy left for outside activities and developed few hobbies or interests. Suddenly, he had large blocks of time which were difficult to fill. He keeps busy each summer, has tended a large backyard garden and enjoys this immensely.

Although he is trying to cope with early retirement, Jon also has made several attempts to obtain another job. At 59 years of age and without any skills transferable outside of steel-making, Jon realizes that his chances of working again are slim. He knows he would probably have to accept a job paying much less than he earned at the mill, but he has been willing to do this to remain active. Some of the places where Jon has applied have indicated his advancing age may be one factor working against him.

During 1978 and much of 1979, Jon and Marianne had to curtail only a few household expenditures. Marianne canned and froze many of the vegetables grown in their garden; and the family seldom went out to restaurants. The couple worried that rising food prices and higher winter utility bills would prove their undoing while on a limited income.

Jon and Marianne both said they would never consider asking for help for themselves. When they did need aid, Jon preferred that Marianne handle all of the contact with public assistance agencies. He said emphatically that, were it not for his daughter's handicap, he would have nothing to do with social programs at all. Asked, in 1981, who had been most helpful to his family in dealing with events of the last four years, he answered: "no one."

At each interview, Jon has appeared depressed. For thirty years, he looked forward to returning to North Carolina and building the retirement home of his dreams. He is discouraged that he will never be able to do that now because of his reduced pension. He does not relish the thought of spending the rest of his life battling Ohio's "hard, icy" winters but does not see any alternative.

Marianne died in September 1979. Jon remarried in 1980. He and his new wife have carefully managed their modest income. By 1982, Jon claimed that he had begun to adjust to retired life, although there were still days when he has "nothing to do." At last contact, the couple reported that they were "spending more than we're making."

Name:	Tom Cinelli
Age:	26
Spouse:	Betty, married 1977 (divorced January 1980)
Children:	Son, age 4 (by Betty's previous marriage)
Education:	High school diploma
Employment:	Unemployed as of June 1980; employed by Youngstown Sheet and Tube Company 1971-1977
Health:	Excellent
Date laid off:	September 1977

At 26, Tom Cinelli was an angry man. He was angry for several reasons; the contempt and hate in his voice were obvious. Tom worked for 5½ years at Youngstown Sheet and Tube as a roll builder's helper. When notified of his layoff status in September 1977, Tom was two weeks shy of marrying his girl friend, Betty. He had very little money in savings, but felt that his steel worker wage would adequately provide for him, his fiancée, and her 4-year-old son from a previous marriage. After being laid off, Tom was eligible for unemployment compensation—but only as a single person. He assumed that once he and Betty were married, his benefit status would change.

Government regulations, however, did not acknowledge his marriage; he continued to receive unemployment insurance and TRA benefits as a *single* wage earner. An appeal filed with the local employment services office was soon denied, leading Tom to many explosive and frustrating moments in his dealing with the employment services staff.

Tom also expressed bitterness toward the several area agencies who have received special funding to study the steel workers or provide them with social services. He felt the money could best be spent as direct handouts to unemployed steel workers. Tom indicated that although he feels it is "all right to be dependent at times" and ask others for help, his experiences with public agencies made him reluctant to request assistance again. He said he felt that a job that paid him enough to care adequately for his wife and son would solve any other problems the family was experiencing.

Betty, 25, and her son, lived in a small, sparsely furnished apartment before moving in with Tom. Aid to Dependent Children (ADC) had been their only income for nearly three years, and Betty had no savings. Their monthly check of approximately $170 allowed them little except necessities. Betty said their food stamp allotment of about $85 per month would usually run out by the third week. Her former husband had left the area several years ago and never contributed toward the support of their son. Betty remarked rather sadly that the only things she had brought to her marriage with Tom were two extra mouths to feed.

Following his difficulties with the unemployment claims office, Tom applied for public assistance and food stamps. He was again denied help with the explanation that his income was considered sufficient for a family of two. Tom told the Welfare Department that while Brian was not yet his adopted son, he had initiated legal proceedings to this end. However, the intake worker responded that, even then, his income would not qualify him for assistance. Tom said he quickly left in anger and disgust with this system.

When he was first laid off, Tom completed the application forms for training programs available under provisions of the Trade Readjustment Act. He was immediately interested in retraining and learning a new skill rather than waiting for the maximum six-month extension period following his first year of TRA benefits. However, through unexplained and unnecessary delays, his application for a drafting design course was not processed until almost six months later.

He felt that had his application been handled properly, his training would have been completed much sooner, and he would have found a job. Despite the delays, Tom obtained his industrial drafting certificate in April 1979.

After the marriage, Tom, Betty, and Brian rented a duplex home just outside of Youngstown. Fully one-half of the dwellings on their street were for sale. Many were in poor repair. The families nearby, though working, earned relatively little, and many collected various kinds of public assistance. Young children played everywhere; in warmer weather, the streets were noisy well after dark. The duplex barely provided them with enough play area for their active son and had little storage or closet space. The parents did not approve of the behavior and language Brian picked up from other children. They said emphatically that they would prefer to move.

Betty learned in March 1978 that she was two months pregnant. She and Tom had tried to conceive for two years and this pregnancy was a happy event for them, despite their financial problems. Betty's mother was concerned with the fact that the couple had no health insurance. When Tom was laid off, Blue Cross/Blue Shield had offered him a self-pay plan similar to his mill policy, but the premium payments were too much for the family's limited income. Consequently, Betty's delivery cost the couple over $1500.

By early 1979, Tom and Betty were close to bankruptcy; they were behind on payments for the car, the color television set, and a life insurance policy. Fully two-thirds of Tom's $500 monthly income was spent on the rent and utilities. Betty said her kitchen cupboards resembled those in the fairy tale: They were literally bare by the end of the month. The family was ineligible for food stamps because their income still was considered too high for a family of three. When Tom completed his drafting design course in April 1979, his TRA and unemployment insurance benefits also stopped.

Despite this, Tom and Betty then expressed hope for the future. Betty seemed to derive most of her inner strength from Tom as he told her over and over (as if trying to convince himself) not to worry, that things would be "all right." Both said they had experienced worse times when single. Together, they believed they could beat the odds. Betty's optimism was evident as she claimed: "Something has to happen, Tom is bound to find a job sooner or later. We're not going to starve."

When Betty was contacted again in June 1980, she said that she and Tom had divorced early in 1980. Betty said that her former husband was still unemployed and looking for work in a nearby city. She believes that Tom's layoff had a harmful effect on their marriage, although she does not attribute their divorce directly to it. "We discovered a lot more about each other during those times after the layoff," says Betty. "It became clear that we just couldn't live together anymore."

Betty now has a part-time job at a local grocery store. She and her son are trying to "make the best of what we've got."

Name:	George Kendik
Age:	52
Spouse:	Carolyn, married 1965
Children:	Daughter, age 15; son, age 12
Education:	High school diploma
Employment:	Employed as of July 1980 as salesman; employed by Youngstown Sheet and Tube Company 1946-1977
Health:	Excellent
Date laid off:	November 1977

George Kendik has lived in the Youngstown area his entire life. Like his father, he began working at Youngstown Sheet and Tube Company as soon as he was old enough to do so. George described the mill as more than just a place to work: it was his life; it served as his reference point, the center of his social activities. George viewed the mill as a kind of "glue" that bonded his life together with those of his friends.

If length of service helped to establish and strengthen these bonds, then George had cause to feel this way. He spent 31 years with the company in "a responsible management position" as a production foreman in the tube mill. George felt his time and experience had been valuable to the company.

George knew for some time that Youngstown Sheet and Tube was experiencing problems. He had been told by his supervisor that "things were not going too well" and that some people might be laid off. To George, the threat was like that of a parent who kept warning his child of a spanking: After continued threats and no action, the child becomes immune to the warnings. George began to disregard the hints of plant closings made by the company and viewed his job as secure.

On November 11, 1977, George was informed that he had two weeks of work left and that he would be placed on temporary, but indefinite, layoff status. The news came as a great shock. After 31 years with the same company, George felt immediate resentment that he would be given only two weeks notice. He thought that he had done the best job possible and that the company should have given him help in finding another position.

George was not alone in his shock and dismay. The news was equally hard on his wife, Carolyn and his family. George and Carolyn made cutbacks wherever they could—groceries, clothes, entertainment—all were drastically reduced or eliminated from the family's budget. Anticipating that he might fall behind in mortgage payments on their home, George went to the bank and discussed his financial situation with officials. However, George and Carolyn were able to manage adequately on George's unemployment compensation, his TRA benefits, and other financial assistance. In addition, they took pride in the fact they, unlike some of their friends, were not deeply in debt. They were able to rely on money they had saved while George was working.

Psychologically and emotionally, however, George was severely affected. For a period of several weeks, he could not even leave the house. He was unable to discuss the situation with his friends or with Carolyn. George was not ready emotionally to begin looking for another job. His confidence in himself had been shattered; he questioned why he had not been reassigned to another division and retained as some of his friends had been. During these periods of depression, he concluded that somehow his best was not good enough; the company had deliberately let *him* go and not others.

George's bitterness toward the management of Youngstown Sheet and Tube became even more evident when he related the effects of the shutdown on others. He told of reading the obituary of an old friend in the newspaper several months after the layoff. His friend had also spent over 30 years with Youngstown Sheet and Tube. He had been, according to George, "devastated by his layoff," and became frustrated and discouraged. Then, he died suddenly of a heart attack. Says George, "I firmly believe that if Lykes had not done this to us, my friend would be alive today."

Not until several months later was George able to apply for other work. In his search for a new position, George was uneasy when his initial inquiry led to a personal interview. While he felt knowledgeable about steel-making, he was uncomfortable seeking other types of work. Before long, George found employment as a salesman in a state liquor store, but with a substantially reduced income and fewer benefits than in his previous job. However, the new work provided a steady income. It also brought tremendous relief to Carolyn who had feared that George might have difficulty locating work.

George and Carolyn's daughter is 15 and their son is 12. Neither is sure yet about attending college after high school; but if they decide to go, George is prepared to make any financial sacrifice that is necessary. George believes that his daughter should develop a marketable skill, something she can "fall back on," if necessary. Perhaps because of his own family's experience, George feels that it is important for a woman to be able to step in and provide for a family in the event the husband cannot. George believes that when his son graduates from high school, he should learn a trade. When asked if he would advise his son to work in the mill, George's answer was a firm "no." "If Sheet and Tube was still in control, I'd say, yes; but with J & L [Jones & Laughlin]—no! With J & L and LTV in there, it's such a big company; they can afford to let these plants go."

George freely explains that he has no intention of leaving the Youngstown area. "If I were 18 years old today, with no family or responsibilities, I would go where the jobs are." But because George has a family, a home, and many ties to the area, he wants to stay. George expressed his feelings toward the area this way: "Some people pick up and leave with no problem. Other have deep roots; it's hard to just pick up and go. I'm the type who likes to stay right where I'm at. If I could live anywhere at all, I would still live here. My church, my family and friends are all here." Carolyn is equally determined to remain in the Youngstown area. She would do "whatever it takes" to avoid moving away, unless her husband says it is absolutely necessary that they do so.

When George worked for Youngstown Sheet and Tube, he and Carolyn frequently would visit the homes of fellow steel workers and their spouses. But the widespread layoffs and plant closings have dissolved this circle of friends. While they still meet informally on occasion, any real communication between George and his friends has been discontinued. As George puts it, "the glue which had held us together for so many years has now become weak."

At last contact, George and Carolyn were "managing," although George's job barely allows them to meet expenses. Their car, which is several years old, is paid for, but they cannot afford to buy the new one they would like. George states that he has "adjusted" now, but is still uncomfortable in a new line of work. He feels that the future is not bright for him. Financially, he feels he will fall far short of the goals he had set for himself and his family while working at Youngstown Sheet and Tube. George is not looking for a better paying job.

Name:	Percy Smith
Age:	33
Spouse:	Rachael, married 1972
Children:	Three daughters, ages 6, 2 and 1
Education:	High school diploma
Employment:	Employed, but temporarily laid off from Republic Steel Corporation in January 1980; employed by Youngstown Sheet and Tube Company 1973-1979
Health:	Excellent
Date laid off:	August 1978; recalled twice briefly

In 1962, Percy Smith's father lost his job when one of the area's largest steel manufacturers closed its Youngstown operation. Percy was 15 years old then and recalls that he obtained his first part-time job while attending high school in order to help his family meet expenses. Within one year, his father found work as a truck driver with a fresh produce company owned by one of his friends. He worked an additional 15 years before declining health and poor eyesight forced him off the road and into retirement in 1978.

Percy says that his father was and still is bitter about his experience with the mills. He remembers that, while laid off, his father argued often with his wife, seemed to drink a lot more than usual, and could barely provide for the family. He thinks that much of this hardship was due to the absence of generous TRA and SUB benefits such as many union workers receive today. His father's job as a truck driver did not pay nearly as well as the mill work, his health care coverage was substantially reduced, and the long hours of driving aggravated an already existing back problem. Percy was relieved when his father worked again. With frugal spending, the family soon squeezed out of financial difficulty.

Percy received his "temporary" layoff notice after working nearly five years for the Youngstown Sheet and Tube Company. Like his father, Percy is bitter. Percy never thought he would experience what his father had. To Percy and his family, steel-making has always been a "top-notch industry," vital to the nation's economy. It is inconceivable to him that another steel mill, especially one as large and profitable as Youngstown Sheet and Tube, would close down. Even after being laid off, he could not believe it.

Rachael and Percy never planned to remain in their present home more than eighteen months to two years. They were unhappy with the poor neighborhood in which their children were growing up and were dissatisfied with the quality of education their daughter was receiving at the local elementary school. They bought the house at a good price with the intention of remodeling it and perhaps renting it to others. The couple prefers to live in the country and had even considered purchasing a beautiful $70,000 home on a three-acre wooded lot, complete with a bass- and trout-stocked lake. However, Percy had not pursued the idea because he had heard that area banks and loan companies considered Youngstown Sheet and Tube steel workers credit risks.

After the layoffs began, the couple's bills mounted. Percy could no longer continue with renovations he had started some time ago, such as paneling the children's bedrooms, replastering and repainting the walls on the first floor, and installing new linoleum in the kitchen.

In September 1978, only two weeks after his layoff, Percy was recalled to work at the mill. As relieved as he was to be working again, Percy's anxieties about his future employment with Youngstown Sheet and Tube did not diminish. Every available man in his shop division at the Brier Hill Works was also back to work by now. In addition, some workers from other divisions (including the Campbell Works) were transferred to Percy's shop to compensate for the loss of those men who had chosen to retire due to age or disability.

With slightly less than five years' experience at the mill, Percy still held about the least amount of seniority among those recalled. And every "twenty-year man" brought in from the rapidly declining Campbell Works pushed him further and further out the door. In the event of another work slowdown or shutdown, he knew he would be among the first to go.

Although Percy could understand the rationale for the transfer, he deeply resented the continuous infusion of men from across the river. Percy recalls his "hatred" for these workers: "I knew those men had families, too, but the thought of mine going hungry and me out of work made me want to kill someone." He mentioned getting into arguments at work with transferred men: several times, the disputes were hotly rekindled after a few rounds of drinks at a local bar.

Percy's wife, Rachael, remembers these times very well. Sometimes Percy would stumble into the house late at night in a drunken rage, yelling and screaming, waking the children. Rachael said Percy would threaten to carry his loaded "Saturday night special" to work with him the next day; for a while, she feared a telephone call from the police or the morgue.

Percy's drinking bouts increased and his bar tabs skyrocketed. Rachel began to scream at the children for the slightest infraction, and she nagged Percy incessantly to quit drinking. The couple fought regularly and violently. In desperation, they opted to stay out of each other's way to avoid arguing. Separation was discussed as a realistic option.

Percy's financial problems did not improve when he was recalled in September 1978. With Rachael's previous bookkeeping experience, the couple devised a careful household budget based on Percy's biweekly paychecks. Their yearly income of $17,000 to $20,000 (depending on overtime pay) should have been adequate to meet the needs of a growing family of five; but Percy began overspending their budget. As Percy related: "It was almost impossible for me to realize how much our income could drop so suddenly, even with TRA and unemployment compensation. I was spending each paycheck like another one would come in the next day."

Thanksgiving 1978 was not a time when Rachael or Percy especially felt like giving thanks. Less than ten weeks after being recalled to work, at Brier Hill in early September, Percy was again handed a layoff notice and told not to come in the next day. This was Percy's third period of unemployment in less than one year.

Percy spent the Thanksgiving weekend roaming through his home in a drunken rage, screaming, crying, breaking windows and furniture, and sleeping intermittently. When Percy threw the family cat out the front door, Rachael took their three children and left. As she later explained, "I didn't know when me or one of the girls might sail down the steps, too." Rachael spent her Thanksgiving tearfully with her parents and younger brothers and sisters. For a time, she gave serious consideration to staying with them permanently. However, Rachael's mother convinced her that "her place was in her own home with Percy." The entire scene was repeated during the Christmas holidays. In January 1979, Percy was again recalled to work.

One source of Percy's anger seems to be his failure to complete a boilermaker apprenticeship at Youngstown Sheet and Tube. In 1974, Percy took a $450 per month pay cut to enter this program. It called for 7,200 hours of training, with the majority of time spent in actual work situations at the mill. An apprenticeship that normally should have taken Percy three and a half years to complete had cost him nearly five years due to frequent interdepartmental transfers and temporary plant shutdowns. Percy paid almost $500 of his own money, taken in small amounts from each paycheck, to cover the cost of the accompanying correspondence school course. He says his school tuition would only be refunded once he formally completed the required hours for the course and passed the qualifying exams.

When he was laid off for the first time, Percy had eight and one-half work hours left to finish the program and had already passed one of the preliminary tests. Although recalled to work twice, he was never able to work in the boilermaker department, and this made it impossible for him to work out his time. Without this single day's work, Percy was not certified, despite repeated requests to the company and the union local for an exemption in his case. When Percy considered how the company "cheated" him out of his certification, his face colored and his voice became much louder. He believes that the shutdown "denied" him his trade.

Percy also connects his emotional reactions to the layoffs with the work situation at the mills after September 1977. Morale among the workers was then very low; rumors of the impending, permanent shutdown passed through the plant daily. Supervision was virtually nonexistent and foremen admitted to having no more reliable information than what they read in "last night's newspaper." Percy recalls that union representatives told the workers "anything" just to maintain a barely adequate level of steel production. Mistrust and anxiety were everywhere.

Facing such a dismal work atmosphere, Percy attempted to find peace and relief in his own home, but with little success. The children seemed to upset him more than in the past. Rachael was frightened at the way Percy yelled at the girls and threatened them with spankings. He occasionally hit them, and this upset Rachael tremendously. Rachael said she, too, became a "screamer"; her own nervous tension stemming from inability to cope with the family's problems. She cried at the least amount of frustration, and after "too many sleepless nights," resorted to "downers" and a little beer in the evenings to help her insomnia.

In 1979, Rachael questioned her future with Percy; yet she wondered what she and the children would do without him. It was not hard for her to recall the warm, friendly man Percy once was. She remembered Percy had always been a heavy beer drinker, but his past drinking reflected a camaraderie with fellow workers.

At this point, Rachael felt a pressing need to discuss her personal problems with a professional counselor. She had tried talking to some of her married girl friends, but they were all involved with their own dilemmas; their husbands were laid off and drinking, too. The decision to seek outside help was a particularly hard one for Rachael to make. Her family and Percy had always cautioned against relying upon anyone else for assistance. Rachael had not told Percy of her intention to seek counseling.

Rachael gave serious thought, also, to attending an Al Anon meeting. Percy refused to consider going to Alcoholics Anonymous. While he admitted that his drinking sometimes caused him problems, Percy steadfastly denied that he might be an alcoholic. Rachael was not sure that Percy was an alcoholic. She viewed her husband's frequent "all-night benders" as a reaction to job insecurity.

In June 1979, these problems were alleviated somewhat when Percy found a new job at Republic Steel. His position as a laborer was a "relatively good" one; but in January 1980, Percy found himself once again on temporary layoff. The couple again had to draw on meager savings to supplement Percy's unemployment benefits.

When last contacted in late 1981, Percy was again working at Republic Steel. He and Rachael described their family life as "about the same" as before the layoff. Looking back on the three years, Percy thinks he might have done better to look for work in another state. He would like to learn the sort of trade that would not tie him to a particular geographic location, perhaps welding or air conditioning/refrigeration work. He considers both of these fields good sources of future employment. And, he thinks that his present job might disappear "in five or six years."

Rachael, however, is opposed to any move that would take her more than an hour away from her parents, since she relies heavily on her mother and sisters for support. She says that while the emotional climate in their home has improved, there are still serious problems. She and Percy and "just hanging in there, for now."

PROFILES IN BRIEF

A Close Call With Retirement Benefits

Name:	Greg Remlak
Age:	64
Spouse:	Carla, married 1941
Children:	Three sons, three daughters (all live elsewhere)
Education:	High school diploma
Employment:	Retired April 1979; employed Youngstown Sheet and Tube Company 1937-1979
Health:	Good, with some respiratory problems
Dates of interviews:	January, March, and December 1979; June 1980

Greg Remlak was employed by the Youngstown Sheet and Tube Company for 42 years. He first began working at the Campbell works several years after graduating from high school. After three years as a laborer, Greg worked briefly in the maintenance department and was later transferred to the railroad (materials handling) department to serve as a clerk, where he spent the bulk of his 42 years at Youngstown Sheet and Tube. Greg retired at the end of April 1979.

Greg and his wife, Carla, are very thankful that they have suffered no hardships as a result of the growing number of mill closings in Youngstown. They described their financial situation as healthy.

Carla does recall a frightening close call in 1978, however. Before the merger of the Lykes Corporation with Jones & Laughlin Corporation, there was a chance that Greg would lose his entire pension because of a technicality. "I was very, very scared," says Carla. "I know things like that are protected by law, but there was still a possibility that Greg could lose everything." Today this question has been resolved, and Greg will receive the pension he is entitled to for his 42 years at the mill.

Greg and Carla have felt the steel crisis in other than financial ways. "You can't witness all we've seen without being affected in some way," says Carla. "All my life I've lived here knowing that the steel industry was the basis for the economy of the Youngstown area. Now I'm watching the industry crumble, and I can't help but wonder when the community will follow it down."

Because they are now in their mid-60s and have a generous pension, Greg and Carla are more concerned with their children's future than their own. Two of their daughters have families and reside in the area. Greg believes that the continued decline of the area's economy will force both of their husbands to search for work in other communities.

Coping With Boredom

Name:	Bruce Stankovich
Age:	26
Spouse:	None
Children:	None
Education:	B.S. in Business Administration
Employment:	Unemployed as of September 1978; employed by Youngstown Sheet and Tube Company 1973-1977
Health:	Good
Date laid off:	September 1977
Dates of interviews:	July and September 1978; August 1979

Bruce Stankovich is 26 years old and single. He grew up in nearby New Castle, Pennsylvania where his father is an accountant. In 1973, Bruce moved to Youngstown to attend college, and he took a part-time summer job with Youngstown Sheet and Tube. Bruce wanted to continue working in the fall when classes started. He discussed this with his supervisor and was given a steady 3-11 shift as a laborer. For the next four years, Bruce would get up early in the morning, attend classes until early afternoon, and then go to work until late at night. His schedule was hectic, but Bruce liked it. He was anxious to finish his college education with a degree in advertising and public relations.

Bruce says he never intended to stay with Youngstown Sheet and Tube. His plans were to finish his education and move West. So, he was not disappointed when, in August 1977, he was given his termination notice as part of the mass layoff.

The timing of his layoff was somewhat unique. Just two weeks earlier, he had graduated from the university. For four years, he had simultaneously worked full-time and attended classes. Now, within a matter of days, he was out of both and had nothing to do. He planned to enjoy the time off and relax for a while. Since he was single, Bruce had few financial obligations—his car, a motorcycle, rent, and groceries—and was able to manage relative easily on his unemployment compensation. He spent his time reading and going out in the evenings.

Looking for the Causes of the Crisis

Name:	Terry Turner
Age:	51
Spouse:	Nancy, married 1958
Children:	Three sons, ages 17, 14, 12 (all live at home)
Education:	High school diploma
Employment:	Employed as of July 1980 as a gas station owner; employed by Youngstown Sheet & Tube 1951-1977
Health:	Excellent
Date laid off:	October 1977
Dates of interviews:	November 1978; January 1970; January and July 1980

Terry Turner refers to his 26 years in the mill as "good years." He explains that he generally liked the work (except for his first maintenance job), and he always tried "to give the company their money's worth." Terry says, however, that most of his coworkers "hated" their jobs; and as a result, absenteeism was always high at the mill. "I know a lot of guys who just called off for the hell of it. They especially reported off a lot in the summer when the heat from the blast furnaces became unbearable, and they went swimming or just about anything."

Terry says he is not sure exactly where to fix the blame for Youngstown's "steel crisis," but he feels that many of the parties involved "just screwed up." He sharply criticizes Washington for not offering greater protection to the U.S. steel industry through controls on imports. Terry also feels that the government owes the steel workers more in terms of benefits. "I mean—every group you can think of gets money for this, money for that. We are the ones who paid for this stuff all along—now who's going to pay for programs that help us when we're out of work?" Terry also takes a dim view of the Lykes Corporation, which purchased the Youngstown Sheet and Tube Company in 1969. "When they first took over, things looked real good for them spending some money and buying new equipment for these old plants. But as time progressed, it became obvious to us that they were taking us for a ride." Terry argues that the Lykes Corporation never planned to maintain their Youngstown operations for more than "a few years" until they deteriorated into a losing venture.

A third group whom Terry blames for the decline of the steel industry in Youngstown is the U.S. Environmental Protection Agency (EPA). As Terry puts it, "They had it out for Youngstown Sheet and Tube from the very beginning." Terry feels that the environmental problems of this area were exaggerated and sensationalized by the EPA, because they wanted to use Youngstown as a test case to "show them they're tough." Terry asks, like many others in Youngstown, "Who the hell wants to swim in the Mahoning River anyways? I mean—it's one thing to want to have clean air to breathe and also clean water, but it's another thing for us to be able to support our families and make a decent living."

In December 1979, Terry and a friend were able to purchase a local service station. His partner provided most of the money for the venture; but Terry agreed to assume the bulk of the management responsibilities. "For now," Terry says, "we are surviving with the station," He hopes that their franchise can become more profitable in the future—if gasoline consumption begins to increase again—but he does not express a great deal of confidence.

Terry has always been quite concerned about the future of his children. Two of his sons have already expressed interest in going to college. As Terry explains, "I would like to see them continue their education, so that they can get a better break than I did. Maybe if I had gone to college and had an education, I wouldn't be in the boat I'm in. All my buddies feel the same way about their kids."

Terry and his wife had always planned to purchase a mobile home and retire in Florida. Nancy explains that "This is still our dream: We want to retire to a quiet life, away from noise, pollution, and bad winters." However, Terry "is not quite sure" how his family and his friends are going to cope with the problems their future in Youngstown holds.

Describing Life in the Mill

Name:	Sam Schmidt
Age:	27
Spouse:	Judy, married 1975
Children:	None
Education:	High school diploma; two years of college
Employment:	Employed as of June 1980 as freight hauler; employed by U.S. Steel Corp. 1974-1980
Health:	Excellent
Dates of interviews:	February and May 1979; June 1980

For six years, Sam Schmidt was employed as a laborer at the Ohio Works of the U.S. Steel Corporation. During this time, he was repeatedly laid off and spent about as much time unemployed as working. "It's hard for me to get a grip on the fact that I've worked at this place for six years," Sam states. "I feel so alienated from the mill." When first interviewed, Sam faced the probable shutdown of the Ohio Works of U.S. Steel and was apprehensive about his future as a steel worker.

Sam talked about the danger of his work in the mill. "All machinery can be dangerous if you're not careful, and the mill is no exception." In his part of the mill, there were many high-speed conveyor belts that moved tons of iron ore per minute. Sam said that most of the employees are cautious when working around these conveyors because they recognize the danger. "But you'll always get the guy who thinks that he knows it all and that safety regulations pertain to everyone but him. We've had guys jumping on belts for 'rides' in which it is very easy to get on but hard as hell to get off." His view is that most of the dangerous situations are created by people and are not inherent in the machines of the mill.

Other working conditions upset Sam. A great deal of iron ore dust was present in the air and was inhaled by workers. "At times, it was so bad that you couldn't see your hand in front of your face," Sam reported. He could not understand why the management didn't do something about this threat to the health of the workers. Sam said that many of the veteran workers developed what they call "red lung," a respiratory condition causing coughing and shortness of breath. He said that even if the mills had remained open, he would not have been around long enough to experience such health problems. "I considered myself just passing through and wouldn't even have considered working there for the rest of my life."

When the Ohio Works shut down, Sam did not search for work immediately. "After all," he said, "I've enjoyed unemployment benefits before, so why not enjoy them again?" Sam explains that he didn't know where he could find work after his benefits were exhausted. However, he briefly considered a part-time job that would have enabled him to complete his degree in computer technology that he began at Youngstown State University in 1975.

In May 1980, Sam found full-time work as a freight hauler in western Pennsylvania. Although the job does not pay as well as his former position at U.S. Steel, Sam is "satisfied" with it. Sam claims he does not mind commuting forty miles to work each day and that he and his wife, Judy, have no intention of moving out of the Youngstown area. Judy feels fairly secure now because she and Sam have put a great deal of money in the bank over the years from Sam's paychecks. She has also "helped a little" through her part-time job at a neighborhood dry cleaning shop. Judy feels that they can live comfortably on Sam's earnings from the trucking job; however, she hopes her husband will be able to get into another trade soon because, as she puts it, "Sam needs a *career.*"

Lost Sense of Security

Name:	Juan Fernandez
Age:	53
Spouse:	Maria, married 1950
Children:	Six sons and four daughters (five live at home)
Education:	High school diploma
Employment:	Unemployed as of July 1980; employed by Youngstown Sheet and Tube Company 1951-1978
Health:	Fair, with spinal arthritis
Date laid off:	October 1977
Date recalled:	December 1977 (went on disability January 1978)
Dates of interviews:	August and November 1978; May 1979; July 1980

Juan and Maria Fernandez came to Youngstown from Puerto Rico in 1951 to look for "adventure" and a better way of life. At that time, Juan began working for Youngstown Sheet and

Tube as a laborer. During the next 27 years, Juan's employment with the mill permitted him to buy a house and provide an adequate standard of living for himself, his wife, Maria, and their ten children. Juan took great pride in his work and felt very satisfied with it.

Life change drastically for the family when Juan was temporarily laid off in October 1977. The couple immediately lost the sense of security that Juan's stable income had provided them, and they worried about how they would manage financially. Juan had just purchased a new car and did not know if he could meet the high monthly payment.

Less than two months after his layoff, Juan was recalled to work. However, he developed a painful condition of spinal arthritis and, by January 1978, was placed on sick leave. Since that time, the family managed to live on gradually declining sick leave benefits and on the modest salary Maria earns as a nutritional aide in a local social service agency. Although Juan has applied for social security disability benefits, his case was denied and he is presently appealing the decision.

Juan has never been extremely active in or concerned with politics; but since his layoff, his interest has increased. He views the federal government as partly responsible for the closing of the mill, because it refused to prevent the import of cheaper foreign steel and steel products. Juan is more suspicious of politicians now, adding that they frequently change their minds on issues. "One never knows exactly where they stand." He does speak favorably, however, of the mayor and governor for their attempts to resolve the local employment crisis, but criticizes the area religious coalition for efforts to reopen the mill under employee ownership. Juan thinks this plan would "harm" capitalism.

While Juan and Maria have had to greatly reduce their standard of living, they do not report any significant financial problems. However, neither of them has adjusted well, either psychologically or emotionally, to Juan's situation; their bitter feelings are still very strong.

Juan and Maria say strong religious convictions are a source of comfort during this family crisis. Because of their involvement in the Catholic Church, explains Maria, they are confident that "things will turn around."

Obstacles to a Career

Name:	Jack Stewart
Age:	27
Spouse:	None
Children:	None
Education:	Two-year technical degree in accounting
Employment:	Employed as of July 1980 as a salesman for a specialty steel firm; employed by Youngstown Sheet and Tube Company 1974-1977
Health:	Excellent
Date laid off:	August 1977
Dates of interviews:	September and December 1978; October 1979, July 1980

Jack Stewart is 27 and unmarried. Following high school, Jack worked part-time for an ambulance company and a local funeral home. During this time, he briefly attended Youngstown State University before completing a two-year technical degree. Jack then accepted a white-collar position with a computer company. Although hired for a six-month period only, this was Jack's first full-time job. Next, he found immediate employment with Youngstown Sheet and Tube as an accounting clerk. He was 21 years old and anticipated working his way up through the corporate structure.

The next two years were very good for Jack. He earned over $14,000 a year, far more than some of his friends with college degrees. He had few financial responsibilities and was able to save enough to purchase his parents' home, which he now shares with them. Jack enjoyed his job and the life it allowed him to lead. In August 1977, he ordered a brand new Cadillac, a luxury he had wanted for a long time.

Jack recalls the staff meeting in August 1977 at which he and his coworkers were warned of impending layoffs in other management departments. The employees in his department were told that their jobs were important and, therefore, safe. Several days later, however, Jack was called into his supervisor's office and informed he had been terminated. He was given his paycheck, ordered to clear out his desk, and instructed not to discuss the matter with anyone. He was among approximately 130 administrative and management personnel who lost their jobs one month prior to the general shutdown notice in September.

Jack was stunned. To his chagrin, his supervisor watched over him as he cleaned his desk, presumably to ensure that no important papers were taken. Jack was "hurt" to think he was so mistrusted. He was especially angered when he considered how he had been "tricked." At his boss's request, he had worked overtime each evening the week before so that his department could complete its monthly work two weeks early. He had complied with this request with his usual dedication and finished his assignment ahead of schedule. But, as Jack sees it, the company "reciprocated" with an immediate termination notice.

In March 1978, Jack gained an interview with a firm specializing in the sale of steel products. Despite his uneasiness about the meeting, Jack was hired and was once again working full-time. The new job paid him nearly $5,000 per year less than he had earned with Youngstown Sheet and Tube, and he was forced to alter his lifestyle and lower some of his expectations. Although he earned substantially less than previously, Jack's future brightened quickly after five months on the job. He broke all sales records in his department and received a personal letter of appreciation from the company's president. Jack remains bitter about his abrupt termination from Youngstown Sheet and Tube, however, and says he would never again work for them, regardless of salary. By 1980, Jack described himself as "secure and happy" and was earning more than he did when terminated by Youngstown Sheet and Tube.

When a City Is No Longer Home

Name:	Gil Reeves
Age:	58
Spouse:	Myra, married 1962 (separated 1980)
Children:	Two daughters, ages 15 and 14; son, age 1
Education:	High school diploma
Employment:	Unemployed as of August 1978; employed by Youngstown Sheet and Tube Company 1976-1977
Health:	Excellent
Date laid off:	September 1977
Dates of interviews:	December 1977; August and September 1978; June 1980

Since moving to Youngstown with his wife and child in 1963 in search of employment, Gil Reeves had worked steadily at Youngstown Sheet and Tube in the masonry department. He was laid off in September 1977 and has no illusions that he might be called back to work.

Gil is 58, a high school graduate, and his only transferable skills are derived from his experience in construction and at the mill as a bricklayer's helper. Gil admitted that he was discouraged about soon finding regular work and he was worried and uncertain about his future. Even though he requested work at some thirty places in the months following his termination, he always met with the same resistance from employers due to his age and "lack of experience." Gil believed he had a lot of good work experience but it is not relevant to the demands of most positions. Despite his age, he claimed that he is in good physical condition with "at least another 10 to 12 good work years ahead."

Gil and Myra originally planned to buy a home and settle down with their three children in Youngstown. For the last several years, they were making monthly payments toward the purchase of their small, but comfortably furnished home in a middle to lower working class neighborhood. However, after failing to find a new job, Gil decided to move his family back to their hometown in West Virginia, meaning that he would default on his house payments and face repossession.

This decision obviously was not an easy one for Gil and Myra. They are both proud and feel they have worked hard to realize even the meager standard of living they had enjoyed. They would rarely consider asking other for any kind of assistance, whatever their need or however minor the problem. Both consider public assistance and food stamps as an utter last resort. This is one explanation for their decision to leave the area and seek work in their old hometown.

Contacted months later, Myra reported that she and Gil had separated. She believed Gil was no longer in the area, although she said she had no idea where he might be. She was planning to remain in Youngstown for only a few more days, as long as it took her to pack and remove some of their furniture and belongings from the house. She feared that the bank would try to prevent her from leaving before their overdue house payment had been made. She said she was returning to West Virigina and intended to work there to help support her three children.

She said that since Gil's layoff notice almost one year earlier, he had become progressively more depressed and moody. While he was "always looking for work,'" the job rejections became more difficult for him to accept. Myra believes her husband's joblessness and their reduced income only served to exacerbate the existing problems within the family. She added that Gil was a rather resourceful person when he set his mind to it, and that sooner or later, he might rejoin his family in West Virginia. This is Myra's hope.

Pride in a Former Job

Name:	Dan O'Leary
Age:	54

Spouse:	Colleen, married 1950
Children:	Two sons and one daughter (all live elsewhere)
Education:	High school diploma
Employment:	Unemployed as of June 1980; employed by Youngstown Sheet and Tube Company 1964-1979
Health:	Good
Date laid off:	December 1979
Dates of interviews:	January and March 1970; June 1980

Dan O'Leary is 54 years old and describes himself as being in "good physical condition." He has lived in Youngstown all his life and is involved in a number of community activities, including some at his church.

Dan began working at Youngstown Sheet and Tube in 1964 as a craneman. Previously, he was employed as a milkman, a gas station manager, an insurance salesman, and a steel worker at another Youngstown mill.

The importance that Dan attaches to his former job at the Brier Hill Works is evident from a conversation with him. "I feel very strongly about my job and that I am a most capable worker." His position did not require any special skills, he says, but "it took some degree of training and learning to really know the job and understand it." Dan was a charging machine operator. He explains: "It is not an easy job, and takes quite a bit of expertise and coordination, and is very dangerous. You can get burned badly if you don't watch what you're doing or understand what you're doing." Without this job, Dan notes, the open hearth furnace would not be able to function.

In the new plants, there are no charging machine operators for the electric furnaces. "They are going over to computers and having computers do the job." He notes that years ago, the international unions were fighting for this modernization, regardless of the cost in jobs, in order to keep plants in certain areas.

In 1978, Dan became engaged in union activities aimed at preventing the Brier Hill Works from joining the Campbell Works in the "Youngstown industrial graveyard." There were a lot of extra meetings to inform the membership of the latest news about whether they would be shut down. Dan said emphatically that these union activities "can only help," because the economic problems of the Mahoning Valley affect everyone.

"But," he quickly added, "We [Youngstown Sheet and Tube] were even denied the right to have our plants modernized!" Dan states that it was not a question of how large a sum to invest, because the Lykes Corporation simply did not want to invest more in their Youngstown operations. There are more advantages to be found in investing elsewhere, he admits.

For the time being, Dan and his wife, Colleen, are enjoying the "fruits" of his fifteen years at the mill: a comfortable three-bedroom ranch in a picturesque neighborhood near Mill Creek Road, two late model cars, and a small boat they take occasionally to nearby Lake Milton.

Colleen describes their situation as "pleasant, but somewhat uncertain." She explains that through her careful budgeting, she and Dan have managed to save a sizeable sum over the years for a "rainy, jobless day," on which they must soon rely. Colleen claims she has no great apprehension about their future, because they have been through "much more difficult times."

Simple Pleasures Become Luxuries

Name:	Averill Thomas
Age:	42
Spouse:	Jayne, married 1965
Children:	Daughter, age 11, two sons, ages 8 and 9
Education:	Two years of high school
Employment:	Employed as of July 1980 by Jones & Laughlin; employed by Youngstown Sheet and Tube 1965-1978

Health:	Good, but suffers from diabetes
Date laid off:	September 1977
Date recalled:	December 1977 (laid off again in March 1978)
Dates of inverviews:	August and September 1978; October 1979; July 1980

After thirteen years in one job, Averill Thomas worried a lot about the future when Youngstown Sheet and Tube announced that it would close down the Campbell Works. By September 1977, when Averill was put on layoff notice, his wife, Jayne, had worked several months as a program technician for a local health spa. There had been a lot of arguments, tension, and threats of separation before Averill finally acquiesced and allowed his wife to continue working. It was a difficult situation for Averill to accept, he recalled; it simply did not fit into his concept of the family unit.

While he was unemployed, Averill found that his standard of living had been reduced. Even more painful to him was the fact that his three children were aware of the family's sudden lack of income. Averill noted that despite the fact that the children were eligible for the free school lunch program, they preferred to carry a lunch or pay full price for their meals. He said his children were conscious of the stigma attached to those students who could not afford to buy their own lunches, and he became more determined not to purchase food stamps as he had done immediately after being laid off.

Averill added that he missed the monthly Saturday movie matinees he formerly spent with the kids and was also resentful that he was not able to buy them an ice cream cone whenever he wanted to. He said it was not the larger expenses he missed so much as the more trivial items that he was constantly reminded he could no longer afford.

Shortly before Thanksgiving of 1978, Averill found work as a salesman in a family shoe store. His employer, while expressing sympathy for Averill's financial situation, could offer his new employees nothing more than part-time work at the mini-mum hourly wage. His boss also made it clear that this employ-ment was only temporary for the Christmas season.

Averill explains that he "threw" himself into his work with a great deal of enthusiasm, and he was soon outselling the full-time, experienced salespersons. As a result, Averill was approached by the branch manager and was offered a full-time position to begin when his unemployment benefits were exhausted shortly after Christmas. He was also suggested as a candidate for the assistant branch manager training program. The money would not be much more than Averill was already earning, but he was interested in the title "manager," which would enhance his resume and make a midlife career change possible. At least, Averill felt, he could "get along" with the shoe store position until he found a better paying job.

Then, in October 1978, Averill was hired by Jones & Laugh-lin, a specialty steel plant in Youngstown. He reported that he liked his job and had "adjusted" successfully to it, although it is "very different" from his former position at Youngstown Sheet and Tube. Averill's main concern was that the job does not pay "too well"; consequently, he and Jayne have had to "tighten their belts."

Despite his more recent "good fortune," as Averill describes it, he does not expect his present job to last. "I think they'll [Jones & Laughlin] close down by the end of the year or early next year," Averill predicts. In the event of a shutdown, he and Jayne would seriously consider relocating outside of the Youngstown area. "We both really like Youngstown," says Averill, "but we may have to move to the South where there are more opportunities."

Although they are somehat apprehensive about the future, Averill and Jayne describe their current situation as "happy," and they are preparing for the years ahead by "saving more and spending less."

Persisting Bitterness

Name:	Ken Siegel
Age:	27
Spouse:	Susan, married 1976
Children:	None
Education:	High school diploma
Employment:	Laid off from latest job as of June 1980; employed by Youngstown Sheet and Tube 1973-1978
Health:	Excellent
Date laid off:	January 1978
Dates of interviews:	July and September 1978; March 1979; June 1980

Ken Siegel is a 27-year-old former employee of the Youngstown Sheet and Tube Company. Ken's family has worked for the steel industry in the Youngstown area for several generations. Ken's father, now 69, recently retired from Youngstown Sheet and Tube after 37½ years of service and only three days off for sick leave. Ken had worked at the same plant for five years and stresses that he is "very proud" of his and his father's work records.

Ken once considered his job as a steel worker a "safe" position: something from which he would, like his father, probably retire. And despite announcements of plant closings and massive layoffs (including the termination of his own job), Ken was confident, for a while, that the mills would reopen in a year.

Ken now has bitter feelings toward the Lykes Corporation and the Youngstown Sheet and Tube management. He feels that the parent company (Lykes-LTV) literally "milked" the Youngstown Sheet and Tube "cow" dry, skimming the best of the "cream" (profits) for itself. He is also quite vocal in his criticism of management's failure to maintain machinery and equipment and ensure safe working conditions at all times.

Ken and his wife, Sue, have been married since 1976. Like many newly married couples their age, they yearn for a home of their own, a place suitable for raising the children they definitely plan to have. For the time being, however, they have decided to defer these plans. They consider themselves lucky for already having bought the house trailer they now occupy in a quiet, residential part. "At least," Sue points out, "we do not have to face monthly house payments." The decision to put off starting a family was not as easy to accept, however. Sue is 33 and feels that she has waited "long enough" to bear a child. She stresses that she feels "cheated" by the mill shutdown and the effect it has had on the economic security of her marriage.

In June of 1979, Ken found a job at a Youngstown steel products company. He enjoyed his job during his first six months of work, but in January of 1980, he found that he was once again laid off.

Ken looks at his family's current situation as "pretty good." His unemployment benefits are good and he has been doing odd jobs to make a few extra dollars. He thinks he is more fortunate than many who worked with him at Youngstown Sheet and Tube. "Many of my friends had just bought houses, and they have lots of kids to feed. I look at some of them and see their situations as desolate," explains Ken. He is very relieved that the same is not true for him and his family.

Adjusting to Unexpected Retirement

Name:	Jim Sedlowski
Age:	66
Spouse:	Alice, married 1939
Children:	One son and one daughter (both live elsewhere)
Employment:	Retired October 1977; employed by Youngstown Sheet and Tube Company 1955-1977
Health:	Good
Date laid off:	October 1977

Dates of interviews: October 1978; January and
                              September 1979; June 1980

Jim and Alice Sedlowski have lived in the Youngstown area
all their lives. When he graduated from high school, Jim became
a clerk for a local manufacturing company. He changed jobs
several times before accepting employment with Youngstown
Sheet and Tube as an industrial engineer in 1955. At age 43,
Jim decided to spend the remainder of his working career with
the company in cost control management. He and Alice own
their home, and their two grown children have left the Youngstown area.

At 63, Jim was beginning to think about retirement. He had
spent nearly 22 years with Youngstown Sheet and Tube and
talked occasionally with Alice about retiring within a year or
two. But with the sudden plant closing, Jim did not have the
opportunity to plan his own retirement; it was done for him. On
October 20, 1977, upon returning home from his vacation, Jim
was advised he had one week left. Caught by surprise, he was
only thirteen months shy of his 65th birthday. By this margin,
he lost the chance to collect a better pension and be eligible for
Social Security.

The first year of retirement was difficult for Jim. The adjustment, a problem for many people, was more troublesome
because of the unexpectedness of his termination. To his
advantage, Jim is very handy around the house and enjoys
repairing and constructing things in his home workshop. He has
put his time to good use by building a dining room table and
chairs for their home.

Nevertheless, Alice noted that it took Jim about nine months
to adapt to his new lifestyle. During this time, he displayed
typical signs of depression. While he really did not feel bitter
about his situation in general, Jim said he would have appreciated
some advance notice of his "retirement."

Alice has been very understanding and patient with Jim and
has taken a great interest in his activities. She encouraged him
to enclose the patio, a task he had wanted to do for quite some

time, and complete other projects around the house. They both feel rather fortunate. In comparison to many of Jim's friends who lost their jobs while still in their late 40s or early 50s, their own problems do not seem nearly as severe. They claim to be prepared to live on less income, because their experiences during the Great Depression taught them how to get along without many of the comforts they have enjoyed over the years.

For the present, Jim and Alice are content with their home in a Youngstown suburb; they have no intention of moving. "We like to visit other cities," explains Jim, "but this is where we'd rather live."

CONCLUSION

These case studies provide insights into the effects of a plant shutdown and the types of coping behavior manifested by laid-off workers that supplement the statistically derived generalizations of Chapter 3. While these cases cannot be considered representative of the total population, it is still worth reviewing them as a group to highlight some repeated patterns of impact and response.

Workers' View of the Shutdown

A number of the workers indicated that the shutdowns had been anticipated for several years. Many of the workers interviewed saw the closings as inevitable because of the failure of the steel industry to modernize its facilities and the absence of federal protection for domestic steel. Still, they expressed shock and disbelief at the actual shutdown announcement: How could the steel mills, which had provided their livelihood for so many years, simply pack up and leave the area?

Workers' Views of Corporations

Many of the workers expressed considerable bitterness toward the Lykes Corporation, which purchased the locally based company in 1969, and the LTV Corporation, a subsidiary of Jones & Laughlin, which merged with Lykes in 1978. Many of the steel workers felt that they had been used as pawns by the large corporations in a long-planned effort to phase out the Youngstown mills. One of the workers expressed his resentment metaphorically by saying that the corporations "milked" the Youngstown Sheet and Tube "cow" dry, skimming the best of the "cream" (profits) for themselves. While some of those interviewed were not as critical of the mergers, the prevailing view was one of suspicion and bitterness.

Workers' Views of the Unions

Many of those who discussed the role of the unions in the steel mills viewed them as relatively helpless. Despite the recognized power of the United Steelworkers Union and its locals in Youngstown, the workers believed union efforts were characterized by a lot of talking and little action. Some of those interviewed pointed out the substantial increase in the number of meetings and discussions taking place in the union halls, but noted that these activities involved only a small percentage of workers and did not lead to solutions. Although the prospect of community ownership for the mills had been extensively debated, the majority did not see this as a viable option because they did not expect such a venture to make a profit.

While a few of the workers complained that the unions had become too powerful in some matters, they expressed regret that their union locals could not prevent the shutdowns.

Prospects for Reemployment

Three workers retired early due to the shutdown. The remaining unemployed steel workers sought work elsewhere but discovered that high-paying jobs were scarce in the Youngstown area. The job-seeking steel workers faced another obstacle: Their limited skills and training were not viewed favorably by most employers in the area. Many businessmen viewed the ex-steel worker as an unwise investment: someone either too old or too set in his ways to learn a new trade. As a result, many of the older workers who sought new jobs found few open doors.

A number of the workers did locate full-time jobs during the period of contact. While many of these were described as "good jobs," they were typically lower paying than their previous work in the steel mills.

Financial Difficulties

Both the workers who had found new employment and those who had not reported financial difficulties. Many of those interviewed explained that they had exhausted their savings and their rainy day funds. Most of the workers also indicated that they and their families had begun to budget personal spending more carefully. Many had foregone hopes of buying a new car; some had postponed plans to have children; and a few had decided not to purchase a new home. While in no case did a worker or spouse describe the situation as desperate, the financial problems were significant for those unemployed men whose benefits had expired and for those who were rehired in lower paying jobs.

A number of workers said that they were making sacrifices to provide their children with something better. Many stressed the importance of a college education and stated that they were willing to give up some things in order to provide their children with the opportunity to attend college.

Some workers said that they had been through rougher times; and others said that they were managing. None of the workers or spouses saw financial ruin ahead for themselves; rather, they typically viewed the future with an attitude that things would get better.

Family and Personal Problems

When asked about their social and family lives, the majority described these as about the same as before the shutdowns. Some recognized the stress the layoffs had created, but claimed that they were adequately coping with it. The majority did not think their financial difficulties had created personal or family problems.

In several cases, however, serious family and personal problems arose that may be attributed (at least in part) to the layoffs. One couple finalized a divorce action and another separated during the period of contact. While neither of the wives blamed her husband's layoff directly for the breakup, each indicated that tensions had been aggravated by the mill shutdowns.

In one case, a drinking problem seemed to be directly related to a worker's layoff. The spouse reported that her husband had frequented local bars much more since his termination at the mill. He often arrived home at late hours in a drunken state, and occasionally would strike the children at the slightest provocation.

While it is impossible to trace the causes of personal problems such as these, it is clear that tensions did increase in the households of some of the laid-off workers.

Desire to Leave the Youngstown Area

When the workers were first contacted, none indicated any desire or intention to move from the Youngstown area. All said they were satisfied with their current homes and with the area as a place to live. During subsequent contacts, however, there was a noticeable change in attitude: Many of the workers and their spouses began to consider moving from the area. Those who expressed this view acknowledged an attachment to Youngstown and a reluctance to move; however, they also recognized the declining job opportunities in the area. Many described the area as severely depressed, a place where the old will live out their lives and that the young will leave.

Of those who indicated a desire to move, none revealed definite plans, although the South, West, and nearby larger cities were mentioned as possible future homes. The primary concern of those who considered moving appeared to be a desire to provide greater opportunities for their children, many of whom were of working age.

Gauging the Emotional Response

While conclusions from such evidence concerning interviewees' emotional states are questionable, it is worth reporting impressions received during the series of interviews. Workers and their spouses usually expressed cautious optimism, a view that their situations would probably improve. However, there was a noticeable lack of conviction and confidence in this idea on the part of the workers and spouses. During many of the sessions, the worker or spouse was quiet and almost sullen in manner, and while freely responding to the interviewer's questions, did not volunteer to elaborate on answers. These impressions became stronger during later contacts, for both those who had found work and those who remained unemployed. At this time, interviewers reported a feeling that things were not the same for the workers and their spouses; that their lives had changed significantly and they were not as happy as they had been prior to the shutdowns.

While such impressions are neither quantifiable nor verifiable, they do provide greater insight into the experiences of the victims and their families of mass unemployment. One final observation of the variety of personal situations and reactions is especially pertinent to the discussion that follows. Given such variations, it may be difficult to develop an effective set of programs to prevent or alleviate mental health problems generated by mass unemployment.

Note

1. The fifteen workers were not chosen at random but instead to represent a range in terms of age and family status. Names are fictional.

Chapter 6

THE COMMUNITY
MENTAL HEALTH
SERVICES RESPONSE

The Youngstown closing not only triggered changes in the lives of individuals, it also brought responses from community leaders and professional helping agencies. Notably, the community mental health center serving the area most affected immediately applied for and received an emergency grant from the state mental health department. This local agency took the lead initially in trying to organize and coordinate a human services response to the economic crisis.

This chapter examines the mental health system's response to the Youngstown closing. The response must be understood as taking place in an ambiguous problem context, with minimal precedent or external guidance as to what actions were appropriate to the situation or who was responsible for taking these actions. Before describing or evaluating the mental health system's response, it is important to analyze the situation that faced community agencies and leaders in the wake of the closing announcement.

CRISES AND DEMANDS FOR SERVICES

It is reasonable to expect that any localized disaster or crisis will produce stress in the lives of individuals and that this stress will be manifested also as a surge of demand for human services.[1] This hypothesis is, in fact, widely held among human services professionals. If the expected surge of demand should not appear, however, many would conclude that a community crisis did not exist. The absence of services demand can be interpreted, of course, in other ways. What mental health professionals and others expect, what occurs, and how it is interpreted all influence how they respond to a community crisis.

Psychological effects of natural disasters and economic crises. It is instructive to both compare and contrast the effects of economic crises with those of another class of events commonly termed natural disasters. Both types of crisis produce psychological and social stresses. However, the intensity, incidence, and timing of these effects varies both within and between the two categories.

Recent studies of the impact of natural disasters on their victims and others in a community generally concluded that such disasters have little lasting negative psychological impact. Taylor, Ross, & Quarantelli (1976) find "little in the way of solid evidence that mental illness increases after a major disaster beyond that which would otherwise exist in the areas." Such data as there are suggest that the belief about severe psychopathological after-reactions of disasters is one of the major myths that abound about human responses to extreme collective stress.

> On the other hand, few would deny that victim populations undergo considerable stress and strain and that they exhibit varying degrees of concern, worry, anxiety, and the like. . . . Only someone out of contact with reality will not manifest some kind of psychological stress when directly threatened or endangered. Disasters may not create mental illness, but they

do undoubtedly affect mental health. The empirical question, as yet undecided, is the degree to which they have an effect. Also at issue is the extent to which certain problems in living occasioned by a disaster should be regarded as mental health problems [Taylor et al., 1976, p. 7].

These authors point to the Xenia, Ohio tornado aftermath. When a mental health services delivery system based on the medical model and an "assumption that there would be demands for clinically based services" was established, "almost no use was made of the proferred services" (Taylor et al., 1976).

To the extent that natural disasters resemble economic crises, they may be similar in their effects and their implications for mental health services. However, the two types of crises do appear to differ in major respects.

During periods of mass unemployment, the affected individuals as well as others may not hold consistent perceptions of the cause of the crisis. As opposed to a natural disaster, there may be no agreement on the agent responsible for mass unemployment. In the Youngstown steel crisis, various individuals blamed the steel corporations, government, foreign steel competition, unions, management, and outdated mills and equipment. Mass unemployment provides no single cause against which to focus anger or rally action. This ambiguity complicates the individual's efforts to understand and respond to the crisis. It also makes it more difficult to design programs that meet his or her psychological needs.

Most communities pull together during a natural disaster. Community efforts are intended to restore or improve original conditions. Quite the opposite may occur during mass unemployment. Emergent groups, as well as extant groups, may vigorously compete. Then no united effort is possible. Even worse, groups may work at cross purposes, regardless of the consequences. In Youngstown, one group wished to diversify local industry and thereby weaken local reliance on a steel-based economy. Another group wanted to abandon the outdated mills and build new ones. Still another group sought to reopen the old mills even if they were noncompetitive. Yet another wished to create a national steel research center in the valley. No unified effort was achieved. This caused worker misunderstanding, confusion, and a loss of confidence in the political system and its leadership (Buss, Hofstetter, & Redburn, 1980). On a psychological level, it can be argued that those groups attempting to help in the crisis may actually make things worse by confusing perceptions and, in some cases, inadvertently raising false hopes. Likewise, human services administrators, who must design programs that balance the conflicting views and interests of various leaders and agencies, may find themselves caught in the battle. The clear cause of natural disasters helps to avoid or minimize such conflicts.

By their nature, natural disasters suggest that the victim is not really at fault. As a result, observers usually are sympathethic to victims of natural disasters. By contrast, in mass unemployment, many observers and laid-off workers place part of the blame for a plant shutdown on the worker. Consequently, the unemployed worker is sometimes seen as deserving his or her fate and not worthy of empathy or assistance.

If a flood destroys a city, chances are that solicited and unsolicited aid will flow into that region. There may even be a problem in coordinating the amount of incoming aid. If mass unemployment occurs, resources may flow to the area to study the problem or to foster new economic development. But, for the most part, funding to address the health and mental health needs of the affected people is limited mainly to unemployment compensation. In fact, one consequence of mass unemployment is a widespread loss of medical health insurance coverage among those at heightened risk of health or emotional problems.

In the case of Youngstown, millions of dollars were spent by all levels of government to study the problem of mass unemployment. Only about $150,000 was provided to the region specifically for increased mental health services. Workers were blamed for high wage demands, low productivity, and poor quality production. Management was blamed for mismanaging the mills by not renovating them, for falling behind foreign competition, for fixing prices, and for incompetence (Ignatius, 1979). Victims of mass unemployment are not viewed in the same way or helped to the same extent as victims of natural disasters.

Community and individual needs are more clearly delineated during natural disasters. There is the immediate need for shelter, food, and clothing. Mental health needs include helping individuals cope until original or better conditions are restored. The implication is that the original or better conditions will be forthcoming sooner or later.

In the crisis of mass unemployment, many do not experience the need for basic necessities to sustain life. Unemployment compensation, finding a job, or retirement may obviate these needs. Nevertheless, they face emotional stress beyond their previous experience or ability to cope. In many cases, it is not apparent how they should respond. The steel mill closings in Youngstown again provide an example. The typical worker has worked all his life in the mills. Perhaps he cannot retire, or his skills are not transferable to other jobs, or he is in poor health because of working conditions. He has children in college and a mortgage on his home. There are no steel-related jobs to be had and few non-steel-related jobs available. Most of his life he has had an upper middle-class income. There may be little in his personal experience that would guide him to an appropriate response.

Finally, many services to victims of natural disasters are provided efficiently just after disaster strikes. This is possible in many communities because administrators and citizens have experience in dealing with natural disasters. Repeated river flooding in a particular community provides an example. In these cases, plans for dealing with a crisis exist (of course, there are too many instances where disaster plans are found to be inadequate or lacking, with tragic consequences). They merely await execution even in communities without disaster experience. The methodology for dealing with disasters is known or can be quickly implemented by outside sources.

Economic crises also warrant an immediate response. This response, however, is not based on a well-developed methodology, as in the case of a natural disaster. There is no established body of knowledge that suggests how the psychological problems due to mass unemployment will manifest themselves or how they should be treated.

In addition, it is assumed that in the case of an economic crisis, there is time to act. Administrators believe the real crisis of mass unemployment occurs after the worker's income is greatly reduced, not when the worker's job is terminated. This is based on the fact that generous unemployment compensation provides a worker with a high equivalent income for many months after job termination. Administrators feel they have time to study the crisis and ensuing problems, conduct needs assessments, and seek supplemental funding. They seek to develop a methodology and set of programs to be provided "when the worker's money runs out." One mental health administrator summed up his frustration in this regard as follows:

> I think that anytime someone is getting $205 a week, delivered to the door, there will be some people who will not do anything until that is going to stop. I think some of these people are going to let the fuse burn right down until there's nothing left and I think you know that I'm very frustrated by the fact that we've tried very hard to offer these programs and we've had minimal response by laid-off steelworkers. We've had all kinds of response by the community in general, but not from laid-off Sheet and Tube workers.

Interviews with the terminated steelworkers suggest that this strategy may not work. First, it appears that many workers and their families are under greatest stress soon after they discover they have lost their jobs. To delay services to those in immediate need until a later date may very well make treatment of their mental and emotional problems more difficult. Second, once workers leave the closed plant, many are hard to locate or contact. As a result, they may never be identified as possible clients in need of mental health services. Third, those who can be contacted are not easily convinced to participate in programs. These three factors, based on timing and poor prior planning, preclude effective service delivery.

In summary, there appear to be important differences between natural disasters and economic crises. The latter tend to be more ambiguous in their causes and the nature and timing of their effects. Consequently, economic crises pose greater difficulties for the designers of mental health programs and other efforts seeking to meet the human needs of those affected.

MENTAL HEALTH SERVICES RESPONSE BY THE LOCAL SYSTEM

The emergency grant. The Eastern Community Mental Health Center, serving the area within Youngstown that was most affected by the crisis, applied for and received a grant of over $100,000 from the state mental health department in early 1978, to provide emergency service to terminated workers and their families.

Eastern consists of one main and seven branch offices serving one-half of Mahoning County's population. Prior to special funding, the center employed one part-time and eight full-time professionals. Staff worked an average of 52 hours each week. Prior to the steel crisis, during any given month, approximately sixty potential clients were placed on waiting lists. Staff were insufficient to provide all the services required.

The additional funding added three full-time clerical workers to the agency. They were hired to deal with the expected increase in paper work. The treatment staff was expanded to include two social workers, one community psychologist, one outreach worker, and one part-time Spanish-speaking psychologist to deal with English-as-a-second language (ESL) clients. This new staff was further supplemented by a new 24-hour emergency psychiatric unit at a nearby hospital facility, which coincidentally began at this time under separate funding.

When the local center requested the emergency grant, no outline of mental health programs needed or objects to be attained was included in its application. Only after the services were actually being delivered in the community was such documentation prepared. The following is a brief description of the programs and their objectives as defined by the agency.[2]

Drop-in center. A drop-in center was established in one local union hall. It was primarily designed to promote contact with workers, make referrals, and offer credit and other financial counseling. In addition to a mental health worker, staffing also included Comprehensive Employment Training Act (CETA) workers and employees of a consumer credit counseling service. The stated objectives of the center were to

- coordinate community groups, community education, and agency responses to the crisis;
- act as a referral point for persons who needed assistance and had no other entry point into the system other than face-to-face assistance; and
- provide assistance for unemployed persons by making advocates available to assist them in obtaining needed services.

Community mental health liaison. A full-time mental health staff worker was assigned to work at the drop-in center to provide outreach contact with union members. The staff worker worked along with the union counselors and other human service agency workers. The objectives of the special staffing were to

- provide a liaison that would serve as an attempt at crisis intervention; and
- demonstrate the concern of the mental health community for the laid-off workers and their families.

Revision of hours. The normal operating hours for the mental health center were extended to include evening hours. Mental health services became available about 70 hours each week. The objective of this change was to

● increase the number of contact hours available to laid-off workers and their families.

Community outreach/organization. This organizing effort brought together experts and interested persons in the community. They would attempt to form and lead emergency or synthetic groups in attempts to lessen the problems produced by the steel crisis. The stated objectives of the program were to

● organize community groups of unemployed persons at various sites, preferably making each site as natural a setting as possible; and
● provide each group with a trained team leader or observer. This leader would aid in assessing and evaluating special problems being encountered by the group. This person also would aid persons with chronic problems by referring them to the main drop-in center for more individualized assistance. He also would relate special concerns of the group to the program coordinator, for further community education planning.

Community education. Publication of the various mental health programs offered by the community mental health center was deemed necessary. This would inform and attract potential clients to the center and gain and maintain community support. The objectives of the program were to

● provide mass media coverage of programs;
● create agency programs that would provide group presentations as needed by each individual community group; and
● coordinate community workshops that would reach a large number of persons, to better inform the community at large of services available.

Agency coordination/in-service training. Since many staff workers of local human services agencies would not have any special experience with the mental and emotional problems of the unemployed, in-service training was developed and provided to upgrade professional skills of their staff workers. The objectives of the program were to

- obtain agency outreach workers who would be willing to conduct community group presentations; and
- coordinate agency workshops and in-service training that would heighten the awareness of the agency workers of the unique problems and situations of the unemployed person.

Crisis intervention center. The mental health center did not have the personnel or financial resources to manage many additional programs that were deemed necessary. Administrators were forced to contract with other agencies for additional services. A major effort in this regard included a crisis intervention service. It was established by contracting with an already-existing crisis counseling, information, and referral agency. This agency handled telephone calls to the mental health center after its normal hours of operation. Workers took messages, made referrals, or provided counseling on a 24-hour basis. The objectives of the program were to

- provide 24-hour emergency referral service to potential clients; and
- provide immediate emergency assistance to potential clients.

ASSESSING THE MENTAL HEALTH RESPONSE

Whether a program is deemed a success or a failure partly depends on the evaluation criteria established for the program (Wildavsky, 1979). Unfortunately, the initial request for emergency mental health services funding and the subsequent quarterly reports did not specify any criteria for evaluating the effectiveness of the services delivered. In fact, when top-level administrators in the local delivery system were questioned about this, they responded that these services just could not be evaluated in this context.

The reports, which were made available to the public, did attempt to gather some data on client demographics and services rendered. But these data were inconsistently gathered across programs and, in some cases, within programs. Outside evaluation by objective observers became extremely difficult. As a result of the absence of an evaluation concern, many questions useful in determining public policy for mental health and human services will remain unanswered.

Where possible, our evaluation of the services delivered (or not delivered) focuses primarily on the number of clients served by each program. These numbers are one indication of the value and effectiveness of individual programs. Again, the absence of documentation and data concerning services delivered and client outcomes precluded a more detailed analysis.

Statistical and survey evidence show that terminated workers made very little use of available mental health services. Analysis began by examining data on client visits to the community mental health centers in the Youngstown area. Statistics should be interpreted in light of the extended hours of operation, new programs and services, and additional staffing.

Table 6.1 shows the number and percentage of workers and spouses served by the agency under its special unemployment program. Results are charted from its inception in April 1978 through March 1979. Approximately 754 workers or spouses visited the agency during this period. Of this 754, 34 (4.5 percent) of the respondents were from families who had a member still working at Youngstown Sheet and Tube; 49 (6.5 percent) were from families where a member was permanently laid off. The figures indicate that out of 4,100 workers who were laid off (49 ÷ 4,100), less than 2 percent visited the agency. In fact, families associated with other mills in the area (Republic Steel

Table 6.1 Visitations by Workers to a Community Mental Health Agency

| | | | | | 1978 | | | | | | 1979 | |
Employment Status*	Apr	May	Jun	Jul	Aug	Sep	Oct	Nov	Dec	Jan	Feb	Mar
Sheet & Tube Working	1.7	7.5	3.6	2.1	7.5	1.5	3.6	3.9	4.1	12.0	2.1	2.9
	(1)	(6)	2	1	6	1	3	3	3	6	1	1
Sheet & Tube Ex	3.3	3.8	5.5	6.3	5.0	4.5	7.1	9.2	8.2	6.0	10.6	11.8
	2	3	3	3	4	3	6	7	6	3	5	4
Steelworkers Others	5.0	0.0	3.6	4.2	3.8	4.5	2.4	6.6	2.7	4.0	2.1	11.8
	3	0	2	2	3	3	2	5	2	2	1	4
Steelworkers Ex	0.0	3.8	1.8	0.0	1.3	0.0	1.2	1.3	2.7	2.0	2.1	5.9
	0	3	1	0	1	0	1	1	2	1	1	2
Other*** Unemployed	26.7	22.5	21.8	27.1	15.0	14.9	28.6	11.8	19.2	4.0	2.1	14.7
	16	18	12	13	12	10	24	9	14	2	1	5
Others	63.3	62.5	63.6	60.4	67.5	74.6	57.1	67.1	53.4	66.0	80.9	47.1
	38	50	35	29	54	50	48	51	39	33	38	16
New Cases	80.0	87.5	87.3	75.0	93.8	73.1	83.3	85.5	90.4	**	**	**
	48	70	48	36	75	49	70	65	66			
Reopened	20.0	12.5	12.7	25.0	6.3	26.9	16.7	14.5	9.6	**	**	**
	12	10	7	12	5	18	14	11	7			
Total	60	80	55	48	80	67	84	76	73	50	47	34

*Data available did not distinguish between workers and their spouses.
**Not reported.
***Unemployed since October 1, 1977.

Corporation and U.S. Steel) used the service almost as much as those from Youngstown Sheet and Tube. No deluge of potential clients, directly or indirectly associated with the permanent layoffs, was forthcoming. This does not mean, of course, that waiting lists were reduced or eliminated; they were not.

Who uses mental health services? Where possible, clients represented in Table 6.1 were identified by sex, race, family relationship (e.g., husband, wife, child), marital status, and employment status. Although the number of clients seeking help at Eastern was too small to permit statistical inferences about clients generally, the breakdowns of clients into categories is revealing.

As might be expected, not one manager or white-collar worker or his or her spouse sought services from Eastern. Steelworkers and their families were the primary users.

Among families using mental health services, wives of steelworkers were more likely to appear as clients than workers themselves. Some 45 clients were family members as compared to 35 steelworker clients.

Blacks and ethnic minorities were much less apparent on client lists than other clients. Only thirteen black and one Spanish-speaking client were noted in Eastern's records.

Employed workers or family members with an employed head of household were far more likely to seek services than others. Some 50 clients were still employed by the steel industry, although not necessarily by Sheet and Tube. Another 9 were retired or disabled. Only 21 were unemployed, and of these only 2 were laid off Sheet and Tube workers.

The drop-in center. The drop-in center in the union hall experienced amazingly low levels of service demand by potential clients given that so many workers used the union facility. During its operation in 1978, only 22 workers sought its services. Of these 22, 2 workers were not associated with Youngstown Sheet and Tube.

This center was intended as an information and referral point to give workers access to the system. It was highly visible and well-publicized. The low turnout rate at the center should have signaled that the center was poorly operated or that client demand would not be forthcoming in the other programs developed. The failure of the drop-in center is thus especially important.

The Community Mental Health Liaison function was difficult to evaluate. No records were kept or were available concerning the number of clients served. During the times we visited the project, no workers were visible anywhere in the immediate vicinity. Union leaders reported that few, if any, workers even approached the drop-in facility during its entire operation.

Evidence suggests that the operation of a liaison function in such a facility may be all but useless during a crisis of mass unemployment. One reason for this is that a worker would be highly reluctant to seek information at such a facility because of peer group pressure. Any worker visiting a facility would be immediately advertising to his peers that he had personal problems, and mental/emotional ones at that.

By virtue of its location, the facility showed the community mental health agency's support and concern for the workers. But, this was not sufficient reason for a facility, in light of the low client utilization. Personal interviews with local mental health agency directors illustrate the problem with on-site service delivery:

> It seems that to get that kind of cooperation from the individual steelworkers, we have to create a focal point that seems to be separate from the existing social service system, but in fact is part of it. In other words, so they do not feel that they are going to Welfare, they do not feel they are going in with those people who are always there. We could set up an entity that appears to be separate but in fact has been coordinated with all existing social service agencies. So when they come in there even though they don't think they are going to the traditional social agen-

cy . . . because they resist going there. Because it has so many connotations. If they thought they were going to the "Steelworker Aid Station," that in fact is nothing more than all these agencies sitting down having coordinators for them, we might be able to come up with a technique.

Here's a technique. I have an office in Local 1418, staffed it, and had signs there that said Community Services Program. We had three people come in six months. Okay, if you want to get together and do something like that, we could have that sort of thing available right in the union hall. I'll give you the office because they sure won't come and see me out there. Because we are identified with "you can't do it, buddy; you lost your job, now you are losing your mind"; we're identified with sickness and weakness.

We have a career testing program setup for anyone who comes in who wants to know aptitude, ability, interests; through the diagnostic and evaluation clinic, they would do a vocational battery and make that information available to any prospective employer free of charge. Do you know how many people we have had? Three! We've had three people take advantage of that service and we pass out fliers, and in the newspapers. I have the same feeling, like, where are the people who need the service? And then, we sat down with Darlene and a whole group of people around the table. And we had Welfare people there and union people, etc. To come up with a brochure: Where can you go if you have this kind of concern? I went on TV seven times and I told people where we are and what we do and here's our phone number, etc. And we're still getting the same people and they're not from the steel mill. They have all sorts of problems, but they're not from the steel mill. And most of them, two-thirds of them, are employed!

I met with a mental health administrator last week about that informal support idea and she brought me up to date on what Eastern Mental Health has been doing. It's really amazing. They started off with a consumer counseling session and advertised it through the union and the local churches in Campbell and Struthers. Nobody showed up. Then, they had one on problems of alcohol. Same thing, they advertised and nobody showed up. She says one of the major problems has been that the union has more or less been in the way: You cannot really form an informal network without angering the union because the union sees itself as official. She said that she went around with the union on sending a letter mailed out that would explain the services available. I saw the letter—it was never mailed.

It is unlikely that the union hall was a good location for contacting many workers, independent of the social stigma attached to mental health service. As one mental health staff worker, whose father was laid off from the mills during an earlier economic crisis period, explained:

> The last place my dad would go when he was laid off was, very simply, the union hall 'cause those were the people who didn't protect his job and he had paid them $20 a month to do that. He wanted no part of that. When he went back to work, they were great people.

Crisis intervention center. The crisis intervention center was the only program that received a deluge of clients in need of services. Figure 6.1 shows the number of telephone calls received each quarter for Eastern from 1976 to 1979.

The data reveal an increase in the number of calls received or made beginning in early 1977, before the Campbell Works closing. After the closing occurred, the number of calls made continued to rise until early 1978. In 1978, the number of calls showed a gradual decline. But, in the second quarter of 1979, the number of calls began to increase. A major question is, was the steel crisis the agent producing this effect or could some other cause be identified?

The center had experienced rapid growth in all of its services during the last four years. This growth appears to have been a function of increased advertisement, especially by means of the mass media. There is no evidence that the services designated to serve the needs of the mass unemployed would not have increased independent of the Campbell Works closing. The

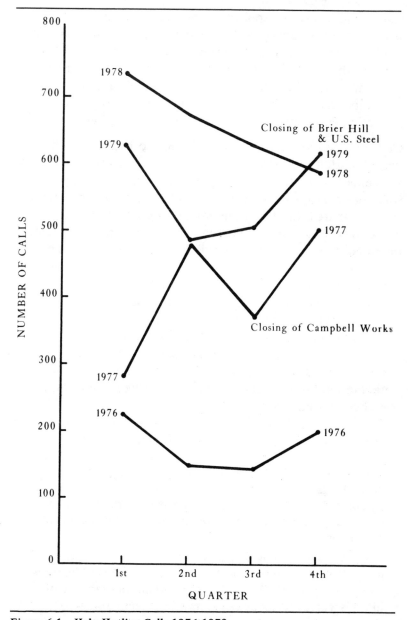

Figure 6.1   Help Hotline Calls 1976-1979

same conclusion also applies for the subsequent closings of the Brier Hill works and U.S. Steel facilities in Youngstown.

These conclusions do not imply that the center is not of great value to this community, only that there was not an especially large increase in the number of persons in the community needing help. Instead, the center has become more effective in attracting and serving those who are in need of help.

Community outreach and education. To evaluate outreach and education programs, it is necessary to measure the public's awareness of mental health programs. This kind of information was not developed as part of the additional funding. Short of such measures, the programs might be evaluated as follows. The outreach and education programs developed and presented in the community were accomplished by community experts. They presented workshops, seminars and press conferences to keep the public informed. These experts were retained on a voluntary basis. They were community leaders and human services workers, rather than members of the general public. No negative impact on the community is assumed and no added funding was required. The efforts were worthwhile to the extent that the community became informed. It is not certain that the time and energy expended by those involved could not have been better used otherwise.

The ways in which the program was perceived by mental health service delivery experts are of interest:

> We're talking about having workers help themselves. Some of these things that were done previously may be done now in a paraprofessional way. It's not the omission of the formal services by any means, but it's just developing a supplement to formal services.

> The process of training lay people to think they're professionals is excellent. The short-term objectives would be to recruit these groups of lay people. Screening is important. In every situation like this where somebody can get involved helping other people,

one can also get the wrong person. We could train a group of clergymen or a group of retired or unemployed steelworkers. A lot of the research has shown that paraprofessionals do not take the place of professionals, but they supplement them.

Another short-term objective is to agree to a location or to contact the church or maybe Community Action Center for a room where we can train ten or twelve people for that neighborhood. I see training little neighborhood groups to stay in their own neighborhood to help.

We're planning a workshop at Eastern for paraprofessionals: how they can help and learn better to understand the problems. Also, very solidly on the drawing board is the idea of a community workshop. In the morning session, we have planned a series of presentations. In the afternoon is a series of "how-to" workshops. Such as, how to have the union help you; how to have the agencies help you; how to have different unions secure positions for you; how to properly use Ohio Bureau of Employment Service (OBES) counselors. I don't want statistics. I want unemployed people to be able to go there and find out how to seek employment. I'm trying to approach this from a very positive viewpoint: that even though these people are unemployed (and they may be unemployed again), they're going to make it. They are strong people and strong people have a way of surviving.

I think we're seeing lots of people relying on their own resources. They're very frustrated and angry at the system, but they're surviving. I think that's the key. We need to go out and assist them in their efforts. Maybe community education would be better than face to face in certain areas.

The program may have had some hidden pitfalls, as one social service administrator points out:

When you get a lot of people passing on information about benefits and what people are entitled to, that's when you get a lot of wrong information. Consequently, people come in with expectations and they become irate when they find out this isn't

necessarily so for them but they know somebody else who got
benefits. That is what I say, the best thing is for the people to
come down and apply. If they give you an indication that they
have problems—financial problems, emergency problems,
assistance problems, etc.—come in and apply.

Agency in-service training. Perhaps the most important effort
undertaken by the mental agencies was special staff training.
In-service training for treatment of laid-off workers and their
families was provided to staff workers at various agencies.
Effects of this in-service training were not documented and
cannot be determined.

The necessity for such in-service training was summarized
by one mental health administrator:

Well, training, which was the only other one we dealt with this
morning. There was one question about how effective the present system really is. Whether the present system seems to deal
with people who are "social paraplegics." People who are very
hardcore in the basic need of services. People who need the very
basic services. We can't look at the S & T [Sheet and Tube]
workers in the same light—they have had viable work experience, they have been tax-paying community members—they're
not possibly in need of the same sort of services you would give
to people who have not been employed—people who don't have
education, people who have additional barriers. We're thinking
in terms of how we have to retrain the staff to deal with this new
target group. We're not used to dealing with those kinds of
people.

WORKER CONTACTS WITH
OTHER HUMAN SERVICE AGENCIES

The programs established by Eastern Mental Health Center
were the primary mental health service response to the crisis of
mass unemployment. However, other mental health or related
agencies, which did not receive funding, were also important
factors because they were also contacted by some of the

affected steelworkers. Client data from these agencies serves to round out the picture of service delivery during the crisis.[3]

Two key agencies that deal with mental and emotional problems were chosen for analysis. Client data for both are examined below.

Western Mental Health Center. Western Mental Health Center serves the northern and western portions of Youngstown and all of the western two-thirds of Mahoning County (Catchment Area I). Western offers a complete range of mental health services to this catchment area.

During and after the closing of the Campbell Works, Western received no emergency supplemental funding to provide services either to the workers or the community. Client admission and termination data for Western for the period 1975 to 1979 indirectly provide some indication of how cost-effective the emergency supplemental funding for the steel crisis was to Eastern Mental Health Center. Table 6.2 shows client volumes for Western.

At the Western Mental Health Center, client admissions increased dramatically from 1976 to 1977. During the first full year following the closing (1978), client admissions remained about the same as in 1977. Only 28 client contacts occurred as a result of the steel crisis. This number is only slightly less than that served by Eastern (49).

This comparison reinforces the conclusion that massive emergency supplemental funding for mental health did little to affect the amount of mental health services given to workers.

Alcohol Clinic of Youngstown. The Alcohol Clinic of Youngstown is a private clinic offering residential alcoholism treatment. Services include detoxification, psychological evaluation, and crisis intervention. Alcohol education classes and out-patient alcoholism counseling also are offered. The clinic has no restrictions on its service area.

Previous research indicates that the rate of alcohol abuse increases in the wake of a community's economic crisis. In

Table 6.2   Western Mental Health Center Data
             (1975 to 1979)

| Years | Client Data | | |
	Admissions	Terminations	Total
1975	1,575	1,096	2,671
1976	879	1,905	2,784
1977	1,124	1,252	2,376
1978*	1,158	871	2,029
1979	1,547	1,324	2,871

SOURCE: Child and Adult Mental Health Center, Inc. Annual Reports 1975 to 1979.
*Only 28 client contacts occurred due to steel mill closings.

order to test this possibility, and to see whether any increased alcohol abuse would manifest itself as greater demand for alcoholism treatment, client data from the alcohol clinic for the period 1976 to 1979 were examined. Results of this analysis are presented in Figure 6.2.

Figure 6.2 shows a remarkable seasonality in the data. This persists over the four years examined. Client intake for 1976 and 1977 was roughly equivalent until the steel mills closed in September 1977. For the next three months (October, November, December), some 339 more clients were seen in 1977 than in 1978. After this initial influx, previous patterns were restored.

There may be several reasons for the fall-off of clients, beginning in 1978. First, since the clinic is privately operated, workers must either pay for treatment with health insurance or out of their own pockets. Since insurance benefits expired for many shortly after the closing, it is unlikely that laid-off workers could spare the cost of private treatment. Furthermore, alcohol programs at the clinic are typically sponsored by area companies, because they may salvage a worker for the company. When a worker is jobless, he may not have the encouragement that would have formerly been supplied by the company. Second, beginning in 1978, the length of stay for treatment was increased at the clinic. This resulted in fewer clients, but in increased

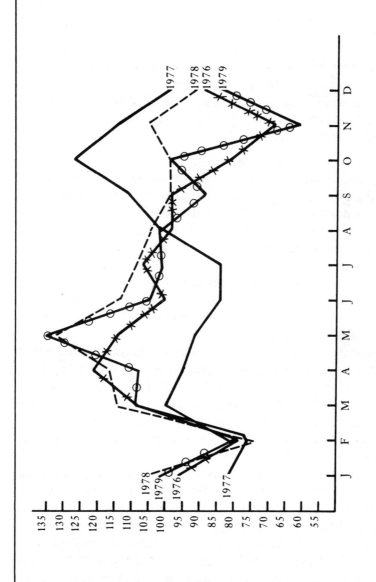

Figure 6.2 Monthly Client Data for the Alcohol Clinic

contact time per client. Third, it is likely that many people with drinking problems will not seek help from any institutional source. The reasons are similar to those influencing mental health service delivery.

In conclusion, nothing in the alcohol clinic data either supports or refutes the hypothesis that alcohol abuse is increasing in the community. But, the initial influx of clients in late 1977 and the subsequent fall-off suggest that alcohol abuse may be a hidden problem that never surfaces as increased demand for alcoholism treatment.

Survey data. Interviews with affected and unaffected workers suggest conclusions similar to those drawn from the available information on program use and effectiveness. Respondents were initially asked: "Have you asked any of the following agencies for help with a problem?" The question was followed by a list of 46 agencies. These included four mental health services, Alcohol Clinic of Youngstown, Mahoning County Drug Program, Western Mental Health Center, and Eastern Mental Health Center; ten employment and human service agencies; and two "catch-trials" or bogus agencies. They were included to identify response set bias.

Only two workers had visited any of the four mental health agencies in the Youngstown area during the six months prior to the first wave of interviews (August 1978). However, the average number of reported contacts with all agencies was three times greater for terminated than for nonterminated workers. Thus, terminated workers were significantly more likely to report agency contact.

The overall level of contact by both groups (less than one contact per individual, excluding employment service contacts) is quite low. It is striking how few of the interviewed workers had contact with agencies offering employment services, credit counseling, and other kinds of nonfinancial assistance. Less than eight percent of terminated workers contacted the CETA or food stamp offices. Fewer than five percent visited any other agency. Explanations might include the absence of need, the lack of needed services, or need not translated into demand.

UNDERSTANDING THE LACK OF SERVICE USAGE

Various plausible reasons can be advanced for low use of mental health and human services. One explanation would be lack of need for such services. And, in fact, few affected workers manifested levels of psychopathology that clearly indicated a need for clinical treatment. On the other hand, even if only five percent of the 4,100 laid-off steelworkers needed services, these 205 workers could potentially place demands on the system that could not be met. Before assuming that this level of need was not present, we should consider other possible explanations for the lack of demand.

Conditions for help-seeking. The question is, under what conditions would a worker be likely to visit a mental health agency? At least five conditions seem necessary. First, the worker must perceive himself as having a problem with which he needs help. Second, the worker must believe mental health services are useful. Third, the agency must not be stigmatized by prior experience or reputation. Fourth, the worker must know where services are available. Close proximity and visibility are important, since the worker would be unlikely to spend excessive time searching for services. Fifth, the worker must be a reasonably active participant in social affairs in general. One must be accustomed to dealing with others in order to approach or make use of any human service agency.

Propensity for help-seeking. An important initial condition necessary to motivate an individual to seek help is the worker's self-awareness that he needs help. But the workers also must feel that help can be provided by a formal service agency. Affected workers in Youngstown were asked: "Have you ever considered visiting a local mental health agency to seek help with a personal problem?" If the respondent answered "yes," he was asked, "which agency?" and "did you finally visit the agency?"

Some 94 percent of the steelworkers in the study reported they had never considered visiting a mental health agency. This group was then asked, "why not?" About 92 percent reported they perceived no need for the services offered by mental health agencies. Another 2 percent reported that the services could not help, even though they perceived a need. Nearly identical results were obtained from spouses of steelworkers and from managers and their spouses.

By default, the identification of need rests with mental health agencies. If workers and their families need help, but are not aware of it, then mental health agencies must develop means for identifying them and attacting them as clients.

Views that people hold of formal helping systems may inhibit them from approaching service agencies (Landesberg et al., 1979, pp. 69-115). Of the terminated and nonterminated workers, 70 percent find it "hard to ask others for help." More than 60 percent "believe grown people should stand on their own two feet" rather than "depending on someone else sometimes." More terminated workers (33 percent) were bothered by seeing the government spend tax dollars on the unemployed than were nonterminated (23 percent). Likewise, more nonterminated workers said it was easy to ask for help (32 percent) and sometimes be dependent (37 percent) than terminated workers (26 percent and 30 percent). A comparison of the attitudes held by the two groups suggests that job loss may reinforce rather than diminish the desire to be self-reliant.

One practical strategy for reaching reluctant workers seemed to be establishing a mental health facility in the local union hall, where many laid off workers gather. As noted, this strategy was unsuccessful in Youngstown. Few workers used the service, even though it was easily accessible. If most workers are unaware of any need for mental health services, and workers will not participate in accessible programs when they are laid off, mental health administrators must discover new ways to identify and assist potential clients. These include new methods of outreach and new modes of service.

Two administrators of mental health programs discussed the problems from the perspective of their own experiences:

> *A:* I think we have to keep trying, but there's another factor that enters in. I'll use the parallel of working with unwed mothers. One of the first problems you have to do is get the girl to admit that she's pregnant. Sometimes she's in her ninth month and sometimes she's in the process of delivering and if you tell her she's pregnant, she's going to be very angry with you and she probably isn't even going to talk with you until she's ready to say, "Yeah, I'm pregnant." I think with the laid-off steelworker, if we go to them and we say, "This is a program for laid-off steelworkers" and they're not ready to admit they're laid-off steelworkers yet, they're not only going to not come—they're going to be mad at you because they don't want to hear that. At the point where they're ready to say, "OK, I'm ready to hear this, I have to deal with it now," that's when you have to be ready to deal.

> *B:* That's a good point. In growing up with my dad, I could see my mother walking around the kitchen moving the dust to see if there were any beans under it to make meals out of it, literally. Many times there was nothing left in the kitchen and if somebody would call on the phone, we were doing just great and usually it would be a very close friend that would buy us food or vice versa, if my dad was working. But, you know, to admit outwardly that my dad was not a good breadwinner, for that family, was just something they were not ready to face.

Experiences in seeking help. What was the experience of terminated workers who sought help from the formal helping system? Workers were asked to rate each agency contacted. "Were you treated with respect?" "Did this help to solve the problem?" There were 141 contacts by 145 terminated workers with the ten most contacted agencies. Very few of these were contacts with the two community mental health agencies.

Their initial experiences in seeking help may have deterred many from further contact with the formal system (Foltman, 1968). Of 87 terminated workers seeking job-finding help from the state employment service, 52 reported receiving help. But, 25 said they were not treated with respect. Only 4 of 12 persons contacting CETA said the agency was able to help. Only 3 of 12 contacting the food stamp office received help. Only 53 percent of the terminated workers reported satisfaction with the way they were treated and effective help from the ten most contacted agencies. More than one-third said they got no help in solving their problems. About 10 percent said they were not treated with proper respect. Again, spouses of steelworkers as well as managers and their spouses reported similar experiences.

Such evidence suggests that initial contacts often discourage further help-seeking from the formal system. To begin with, if people are accustomed to self-sufficiency and unfamiliar with the structure and rules of the system, their first contacts with service agencies may often be their last.

Other evidence of the nature and extent of treatment received by workers was gathered by interviewing case workers who dealt with workers as clients. Interviews with mental health and other human service agency staff members led to the following conclusions concerning treatment. In general, workers probably did not receive the respect they expected nor the help they required. Several reasons were cited for this. First, many workers visited agencies with the expectation that they would receive job leads or come away with a job in hand. When this expectation was not fulfilled, workers came away from the agency feeling they had been treated poorly. One mental health staff member, experiencing deep frustration, commented: "I've met about a dozen people that I had to tell to go back (to the state employment service) because they stopped going once they stopped getting their checks. They couldn't figure out why they needed to go anymore. A lot were really disgusted in terms of going on job interviews and applying for a job *when it's been filled the week before.*"

Second, many staff members were not aware of services and programs offered by other agencies. Some were not aware of services and programs offered in their own agency. Workers were misdirected from one office to another until they became frustrated and dropped out of the human service delivery system.

Third, many workers were upset with government for not responding to their needs. Some approached agencies with chips on their shoulders. The ensuing experience often was unproductive.

Fourth, many former full-time workers had never been unemployed. They had worked in economically stable industries and had good work records. These workers did not feel comfortable dealing with public agency staff and bureaucratic routine (see also Lipsky, 1980). The impersonal treatment, the stand in line or take a number and wait system, and a range of similar experiences led workers to perceive a lack of respect from service agency staff.

In summary, many workers wanted jobs from the human service system, including mental health-related services. They were not interested in changing their lifestyles or accepting lower status employment. As one administrator commented:

> It seems the greatest source of feedback in terms of what is going on in the community is your direct line workers in any agency or any given system. What I'm hearing from direct line staff is that many people who are unemployed or laid off as a result of the closing are very resistant to entering any social service system: (1) they don't want to be retrained, they're resistant to training; (2) they don't want to work for less than what they're already making, and they're indignant at the fact that you offer them a position or a job that pays less than what they had been receiving for over a number of years.

Peer group influence. Another factor that may influence whether individuals visit an agency is peer group pressure. Respondents were asked: "Have you ever tried to convince another worker that any government agency would be of little help to him in solving personal or employment problems during the steel crisis?" Respondents also were asked: "Has anyone tried to convince you that any government agency would be of little help?" These questions were followed by open-ended questioning concerning which agency was not helpful and why the worker tried to convince others not to use services. The purpose of these questions was twofold: (1) to measure the respondent's attitude about an agency (or agencies); and (2) to assess the extent of peer group pressure.

Results were that nearly ten percent of the workers and managers in the sample reported having attempted to convince other workers that government agencies were of little help in personal problem-solving. Reasons offered by these workers were evenly divided into two categories. First, the agencies typically do not solve personal problems. Second, the agencies give clients the run-around. When workers were asked if anyone had tried to convince them not to visit an agency, again only nine percent reported such attempted influence. Interestingly, no one reported being told that a mental health agency should not be visited.

Responses to both of these questions hold important implications for mental health and other human service delivery. If this set of responses is projected to the entire population of laid-off steelworkers, perhaps 300 to 500 workers had a negative attitude about government agencies. They also were likely to attempt to influence others in the same way. Those who reported others had attempted to change their attitude also number from 300 to 500 workers. If information of this kind is passed from person to person over time, it is not surprising to learn that programs for the unemployed are greatly underutilized. Research is needed on how this flow of negative information among workers influences help-seeking.

Negative information flow is not the only effect of peer group influence. Attempts at helping workers who have been gathered into groups sometimes fail simply because individuals are being treated en masse. As one administrator states:

> I think any time you're trying to find out what a person wants to do with his life you're better off dealing on a one-to-one basis because in a group, he's either not going to open his mouth or he's going to go along with what his buddies say they want to do.

Awareness of agency location. Another precondition for service use is awareness of mental health agencies and their services. Respondents initially were asked: "Where is the closest place to your home where you could get help with a serious personal problem—such as not being able to sleep at night, fighting with the family, or being emotionally upset?" and "Where is the mental health center closest to your home?" The locations offered were verified to see whether or not they matched those of the mental health agencies.

Only five percent of the workers and none of the managers reported that they would visit a mental health agency for serious personal problems. But, on the follow-up question, at least seventy percent of the workers and managers were able to name the mental health center nearest their home. Thus, information about agency locations was not the major factor inhibiting workers from contacting mental health agencies.

Social integration. Willingness to seek services from a helping agency or helping individual may be part of a more general propensity to participate in social activity. If an individual did not attend union meetings; was not a member of community organizations; did not participate in meetings about the steel crisis; did not communicate with public officials; did not attend movies, sporting events, concerts, plays, and participate in activities involving others, this individual was unlikely to come out of social isolation and approach a human services agency.

Questions were asked relating to each of the types of social activity named above.

Workers reported participating in the above social activities to varying degrees. As noted, only about 10 percent regularly attended union meetings. Some 45 percent reported they never attended a union meeting. Amusement/entertainment-oriented activities fared somewhat better: 33 percent regularly attended sporting events; 32 percent attended movies; and 21 percent went to a concert, play, or museum. Workers participated in the steel crisis activities to varying degrees: 43 percent attended rallies, 14 percent wrote letters to public officials, and 12 percent spoke directly to public officials about the crisis. About 35 percent were members of social organizations in the community. Although most people participated in at least one of these activities, a significant minority of workers appeared to be socially isolated. These workers were less likely to approach human service agencies of any sort.

ALTERNATIVES TO THE FORMAL SYSTEM: OTHER HELP-SEEKING

If the workers were reluctant to seek help from the formal system, were they willing to obtain assistance from friends, relatives, and other people they knew? Both terminated and nonterminated workers were asked: "When times are hard, some people turn for extra help to friends, to relatives, to social agencies, to groups, and so on. In the last six months or so, have you asked for extra help from any of the following?" Approximately 20 percent of those steelworkers interviewed, both terminated and nonterminated, indicated that they sought help from immediate family and other close relatives. The only other class of persons contacted by 10 percent of either group was the "bank/finance company," reportedly contacted by 14 percent of the terminated and 9 percent of the nonterminated workers. "Friends" were contacted by 12 and 19 percent, respectively. Coworkers, union, clergy, doctor, teacher, neighbor, lawyer, employer, someone you owe money, a politician, and others were all contacted by less than 10 percent of the terminated employees. Interestingly, the nonterminated workers reported that they sought help from friends, immediate family, close relatives, coworkers, union, family, doctor, neighbors, lawyers, and "someone you work for" more often than did the terminated employees. These data show that terminated workers were less likely than nonterminated workers to have asked extra help from friends, neighbors, and coworkers. In fact, terminated workers tended to seek help more often than the nonterminated workers from only one source: the lending agency. Greatest reliance was placed by both groups of workers on their immediate families and other close relatives. Financial problems were the explicitly stated motivation of 30 to 50 percent of the terminated workers who sought out these personal and traditional helpers.

Surprisingly, the terminated workers were more reliant than others on the formal helping system. But, their circumstances did not produce increased reliance on the formal network of social support or on such traditional helpers as the clergy, family doctor, or politician. Under this form of stress, workers did not see the need for or were reluctant to ask for help from others, *especially* from those they knew best.

Efforts at self-help. Unemployment seems to bring out the resourcefulness of some laid-off people as this anecdote from a mental health administrator reveals:

> I met with neighbors of mine who are unemployed but who do part-time work out of their homes. They had skills such as carpentry and they're doing home improvements, etc. One guy did everything he could to fix up his home and now he's working for relatives. It's hard to get a profile of the individual we want to help or to start a self-help group. They're very independent, many don't want help or won't admit they're scared. I talked to a group of four unemployed steelworkers, sort of an informal get-together in my house, and one neighbor still gets called out to

work every so often. His friends told him since he's close to retirement age, he should transfer to Indiana Harbor. But, he isn't about to transfer; he has a lawnmower shop set up in his garage—it's handy that way, he picks up some extra money.

But, tragic examples can be found of workers who cannot cope either in the formal or informal helping system or on their own. Evidence of such cases is given by a social worker:

For the seven people I've seen since the beginning of October, the biggest, most pressing problem has been food. The Samaritan House has been helping me out with two of them. I managed, through my own church, to get a food order through to one of them. One of them had a terrible cold and through Samaritan House managed to come up with the dollars for prescriptions from the clinic at St. Elizabeth's Hospital. One of the church members and I talked of this kind of social service and how to get the public workshop going. We started talking about what kinds of assistance can be given. One hundred and sixteen dollars ($116) per month isn't going to be enough just to sustain the mortgage, so they might as well adjust to the fact of the house being sold. I don't know if that's the right or wrong way—it's the realistic way, I'm sure. There has to be something more that can be done.

LESSONS FROM YOUNGSTOWN'S RESPONSE TO MASS UNEMPLOYMENT

The Youngstown community mental health agencies and others responsible for meeting the human needs generated by massive unemployment, faced a difficult task in the wake of the steel mill closing. There were conflicting perceptions of the level and nature of need. Few models or precedents were available for response to such a crisis. Only limited additional funds were provided to a services system already at or over capacity. And, perhaps more important, the formal assignments of agency responsibility did not match well with the new needs being generated by job losses among experienced workers.

The inappropriateness of the resulting response is reflected by worker reactions of indifference and avoidance. While a minority of workers did seek various kinds of formal assistance, their contacts with the agencies all too frequently discouraged further help-seeking. Nor, for the most part, did the unemployed turn to relatives and friends. The most common, short-term responses of the affected workers appear to have involved self-reliance. It would be useful to know more about the personal strategies followed by workers who coped successfully with the loss of work. However, it would be even more helpful to learn more about the problems, attitudes, and behavior of the smaller group of workers who did not cope so well with job loss and yet did not seek the help of anyone.

The first lesson to be drawn from Youngstown's response to mass unemployment is that too little is known about how to meet the mental health needs generated by such crises. More positively, the evidence of this and previous research provides a basis for the tentative fashioning of a more effective community response to mass unemployment.

Notes

1. The President's Commission on Mental Health (1978), for example, estimates that about 15 percent of the population may require mental health services. In the SMSA (standard metropolitan statistical area) most affected by the mill closing, some 80,000 persons might need mental health services.

2. No comprehensive set of program descriptions, goals, and objectives has ever been produced by the agency to document its activities and intentions. This outline was pieced together from quarterly progress reports by the agency to the 648 Board and District XI of the Ohio Division of Mental Health.

3. One important service, which is directly related to mental health services, was the local state mental hospital and associated private hospital in-patient programs. We have analyzed records available for these services, but have elected to report the

results in a forthcoming publication. The recent trends in deinstitutionalization of the mentally ill, reductions or increases in hospital beds, alternative drug therapy, and changes in patient treatment made our analysis much too complex and lengthy for inclusion here. In fairness to this issue, we decided to present the analysis elsewhere in its entirety.

Chapter 7

COMMUNITY
MENTAL HEALTH
SERVICES POLICY

The public response to an economic crisis should include a major effort to reemploy workers and to expand the job base of the community. However, these form only part of an appropriate response. Other parts of a comprehensive services strategy should be efforts by public and private mental health and human services agencies, volunteers, business, and labor designed to help individuals losing jobs, their families, and others affected by the spread of economic impacts. A comprehensive strategy should have two goals: (1) reducing the short-run incidence and severity of financial and emotional stresses, and (2) helping people cope in ways that increase their longer run chances of achieving their personal goals.

TOWARD A MENTAL HEALTH SERVICES POLICY
FOR MASS UNEMPLOYMENT

The design of a mental health services strategy for massive localized unemployment is constrained by the characteristic circumstances of such a crisis. First, the nature of economic crisis makes it difficult to design and carry out effective programs to assist those affected. Second, there is virtually no body of theory or clinical practice to guide communities in designing successful interventions. And third, the usual local pattern of fragmented, uncoordinated, and underfunded human services is an unpromising organizational and resource base from which to launch innovative programs. Planning a mental health services strategy, therefore, will require a major investment of time and energy. The leadership and coordination of this planning effort can come from several sources, one of which is a community mental health agency.

Nature of economic crises. Our research suggests that economic crises develop in ways that tend to complicate the planning process. First, their effects develop slowly, are geographically diffuse, and may be apparent only after months or years have passed. Second, the people most harmed by economic changes are not necessarily those experienced workers whose jobs are first eliminated but others with fewer financial resources and less social support. Third, the people directly affected are, for the most part, emotionally healthy and resourceful people whose service needs, if any, are limited. This group of potential clients is very different from the clientele normally seen by mental health centers and many other service agencies. Finally, there is evidence that the shock, shame, or stigma experienced by many people due to job loss, unemployment, reduced income, or dependency causes them to conceal the true extent of their problems from others. For this and other reasons, those affected will not seek and will show little interest in the help offered by mental health centers or other agencies.

As a consequence, mental health service agencies will not experience a surge of demand for their services in the months following a major plant closing. To get a truer indication of developing problems, service planners may need to monitor sensitive indicators of emerging distress such as calls to emergency hotlines or reports of child abuse. However, these indicators are difficult to interpret and may provide false signals. A lack of visible, immediate suffering may lead planners to misjudge the true extent and nature of the stresses produced, so that they fail to react. Wiser communities will use this time to plan and organize an effective postcrisis response.

The knowledge base. Dooley and Catalano (1980, p. 463) have developed a model establishing the major linkages between economic change and behavioral disorder. They suggest that economic change eventually leads to functional or dys-functional individual life changes. Positive or negative aspects of individual change are mediated by level of social support and coping abilities. Those who lack sufficient levels of social support and coping abilities will manifest stress symptoms. Stress is in turn mediated by such things as access to treatment, family relations, community responses, and so on. If stress is not controlled, behavioral disorders will be likely to emerge.

At each link in the causal sequence beginning with economic change and ending with the onset of individual behavior disorder (Dooley and Catalano, 1980, p. 463), it is possible to intervene with some program designed to break or weaken the causal chain. The earliest and most problematic intervention would be an organized effort to prevent economic changes that are likely to cause widespread harm. On an individual level, it is possible to intervene at any time prior to job loss to inoculate someone against the harmful effects of such an event. After an economic shock, programs may be devised either to provide temporary financial assistance, bolster social support, or to provide coping skills. Still later interventions may take the form of financial support or treatment of individual psychological stress symptoms. And ultimately, interventions may include treatment of those who sooner or later suffer severe emotional or other harm. The public may also be called upon to pay a large part of the social and economic costs of the loss of a productive individual. At the present time, there is little information to guide local planners in determining which interventions will be most cost effective. Consequently, community planners trying to design an intervention strategy should conduct their own analysis of the probable costs and likely relative effectiveness of interventions being considered.[1]

Resources and organization. Although community mental health and other agencies have potential capacity to assist with the problems created by economic crisis, their actual capacity is likely to be limited both by their existing caseloads, which currently absorb most or all of their funding and staff time, and by the current orientation of their progams and outreach/intake procedures, which may give priority to those who are easiest to serve because they have readily identifiable problems. In the case of mental health agencies, these typically include a high population of those with severe disorders or who are chronically ill. However, the bias toward serving people who are manifestly in crisis, rather than promoting prevention, is common to most human service agencies. There are several reasons for this orientation, including the belief that problems posing a more immediate threat to the individual or to others' well-being deserve priority; the bias of professional training, funding, and theory toward crisis intervention rather than prevention; and finally, the ease of identifying and locating people in personal crisis, in contrast to the difficulty of identifying those merely at risk.

Ironically, in times of economic crisis it is likely that local service agencies will experience reductions rather than gains in funds and program capacity. Because there are no mental health service programs aimed at localized economic crisis and few such state programs, any augmentation of services' budgets from these levels typically will be small and ad hoc. Such help may be offset by declines in local support due to the economic pressure on government budgets. For example, in 1981 and 1982, funding for local community mental health programs in

Detroit, then experiencing the nation's most severe unemployment, was reduced to such an extent that most programs were targeted toward recently deinstitutionalized mental health patients, rather than to the unemployed or underemployed.

In such circumstances, it is appropriate to ask whether the recently unemployed should be given priority over other populations. There are nearly always individuals in the community with needs equal to the recently unemployed but who would not be served by a program that is targeted to a newly terminated group of workers.

Aside from the problem of resources and priorities, there are other organizational barriers to effective action. In most, if not all, U.S. communities, the mental health and human services system is both complex and poorly integrated, reflecting a diversity and fragmentation of funding sources, authority and accountability, geographic jurisdictions, and professional orientations (Redburn, 1977; Polivka et al., 1981). The structure of the local services system may bewilder professionals who work within it almost as much as persons seeking help with a problem. Economic crises may provide opportunities to focus community attention on such chronic organizational problems.

Despite its complexity, the local services system does not necessarily offer an array of programs appropriate to the needs of terminated workers and their families. Our research has shown that there is a poor match between the service needs of displaced workers and the programs of local service agencies. Services, outreach efforts, and eligibility criteria must be reoriented before the system can efficiently meet needs flowing from an economic crisis. It will be difficult for providers and their funding/supervising agencies to agree on who should take responsibility for financing, administering, and delivering the nontraditional services called for at such times. Also, because agencies lack experience with administration and delivery of these nontraditional services, they will face significant start-up costs for training, new procedures, and the sorting out of roles and relationships.

PREPARING A MENTAL HEALTH
SERVICES RESPONSE

An effective mental health services response will be one that recognizes the distinctive needs produced by sudden, massive layoffs of experienced workers and, accordingly, includes (1) new outreach techniques to provide early identification and intervention to prevent severe personal crisis; and (2) innovative service programs, going beyond the normal responsibilities (although not the capacities) of local service providers. Implementation of such programs will require a redirection of expenditures and a reorientation of staff and administrative procedures.

Given the needs of affected workers and their families, the greatest benefits are likely to result from actions that protect self-esteem, provide coping skills, and give access to resources. An example would be the training of unemployed workers for roles as information-givers and network-builders; work for which they could be paid and which would build both their capacities and those of former colleagues *without* implying dependency. Given the diversity of individual situations and the variety of services required to meet this diversity, many agencies and actors should be part of a mental health service strategy to aid those under temporary stress. Moreover, the state of theory and practice call for an experimental non-dogmatic approach to designing and implementing a response. More specific recommendations follow.

Prelayoff intervention. When a plant closing or layoff has been announced or can be predicted in advance, the company and union can be contacted and asked for assistance in preparing workers for the period of stress that is to come. The weeks before layoffs occur are a critical time for two reasons: first, because this is a period of uncertainty and anxiety, complicated by often inaccurate rumors; and second, because it is the last chance to reach the whole group of workers at one time.

Catalano and Dooley (1979) argue that "employer-sponsored 'stress inoculation' programs offer an ideal setting for reactive primary prevention among those workers likely to be affected by a company's economic fortunes." Their idea is that such programs could include (1) *education,* making workers aware of the social and psychological as well as the economic consequences of job loss, helping them realistically assess reemployment prospects, and informing them about mental health and other social services; (2) *cognitive restructuring* to reduce the stigma of job loss and protect self-esteem; and (3) *behavior training,* to provide such coping skills as relaxation, stress avoidance, and skills needed for active efforts to overcome the effects of job loss, including job search skills.

Few U.S. companies or unions have given much attention to preparing workers for termination.[2] In contrast, it is standard practice for the British Steel Corporation to give workers at a closing plant individual counseling on reemployment and training opportunities, and on how best to protect their severance payments. The British steelworkers are also given written information on social services and arrangements are made for later, periodic follow-up contacts by a team of counselors (Buss & Redburn, 1981).

Assessing service needs and capabilities. Because communities may misjudge the true extent and nature of stresses produced by massive job losses, a formal needs assessment should be undertaken to (1) monitor developing and spreading impacts; (2) forecast specific service needs; and (3) evaluate the local services system's capacity to meet present and projected needs generated by economic crisis. The product of this assessment should ideally be a document that identifies gaps in the present structure of programs and services.

Communities that lack the capacity to undertake a formal, continuing needs assessment should seek the help of researchers and planners in designing and conducting an appropriate impact assessment. As we have seen, there is enough variation among communities and the circumstances surrounding job loss to make total reliance on studies of past plant closings unwise. For example, the Youngstown closing mainly affected experienced, highly paid, homeowning steelworkers and managers who were almost entirely male, highly skilled in specialized occupations, typically older, and married. The 1981 closing of the Robertshaw Corporation in western Pennsylvania, on the other hand, affected several thousand workers who were mainly female and younger. Moreover, prevailing economic conditions were far less favorable for the Robertshaw workers as they sought new employment. The needs of these two groups of workers and the abilities of their communities to help them are very different. Any effort to develop a mental health services response is likely to benefit greatly from accurate data on the true extent and nature of the economic crisis and an objective assessment of the local mental health services system's strengths and weaknesses. State agencies may be in the best position to develop such needs assessment capabilities and apply them quickly whenever and wherever needed.

Planning. A major plant closing or similar event demands coordinated planning at the local level. Community leaders can use the usually brief interval during which people are highly focused on the needs of the unemployed, more willing than usual to subordinate parochial interests, and willing to devote substantial energy to problem-solving to initiate analysis and discussion. The best persons to convene and lead the mental health/human services planning process may be top officials of local (county or city) government. Because these officials' responsibilities span a range of services and because they have the authority and visibility needed to start up a serious effort of this type, their early involvement is likely to help agencies transcend their narrower interests. Representatives of state government may play a similar role. Although they may not participate in the detailed design of a services strategy, local or state government leaders must ultimately make the decisions that will put a strategy into action. The mayor or county executive may be called upon to clarify agency responsibilities, approve funds for new programs, negotiate with higher levels of government over the benefits and services available to terminated workers, or support emergency tax levies if need be.

Regardless of its leadership, a planning group should be composed of persons representing various local government and voluntary sector mental health/human services agencies. This group should oversee the detailed planning of a comprehensive services strategy. The group's exact composition will vary depending on local jurisdictional patterns and the nature of existing provider councils. However, we believe that it should in all cases include the state employment service, principal job-training agencies, community mental health agencies, and representatives of health and privately-funded social welfare agencies. Where an active comprehensive human services provider council exists prior to the crisis, it may serve as the vehicle for planning a response; if such a council does not exist, the crisis may well bring it into existence (Taber et al., 1979; Buss & Redburn, 1980). Since authority typically is fragmented and responsibility for organizing and delivering the needed services is unclear, only determined efforts to construct a comprehensive, workable services strategy will produce effective action.

REACHING THOSE IN NEED OF HELP

As shown in the preceding chapter, many laid-off workers do not perceive a need for formal helping services, do not use them regardless of need, and do not think highly of the services they might receive. In addition, mental health services are embedded in a larger maze of agencies with diffusely defined functional responsibilities. This complex structure is confusing to people who, for the most part, have never used formal services before, that is, laid-off workers who lack bureaucratic competence. It is also likely that agencies will be scattered geographically, so that some services may be too distant from workers they are supposed to serve. In contrast to the problems of formal service delivery as noted aove, informal self-help or social networks constitute a second possible source of the support required by workers in times of need. These informal sources of support include families, friends, churches, and so on. The outreach and communication roles to be played by formal and informal helpers need both definition and coordination.

Clearly, the problem of delivering mental health services to those in need has two possible solutions: transform either the delivery system or the clients. It is far easier and, we believe, more beneficial to transform the delivery system.

Centralized access point. A central, noninstitutional access point should be created through which workers can be referred to *all* community services. Access to services would include everything from daycare centers through consumer credit and financial counseling to psychological therapy. It is important that the access point be noninstitutional. Such an access point could be staffed by workers well-versed in diagnosing and referring unemployed workers and their families to appropriate programs or treatments. It is necessary also to have the support of union leadership for this project where workers are organized. It is useful to employ laid-off workers in the project as well. They are likely to be sensitive to the needs of their friends and former coworkers, they know where to locate them, and they might know how to approach them.

Other outreach programs. One manifestation of community mental health outreach programs is a centralized access point for service delivery or referral. Others include small satellite or store-front offices liberally scattered in the community. Geographic dispersal moves agencies closer to workers at least spatially. It does not, however, remove other barriers that hamper delivering services to those who need them.

One way to solve this problem might be for one individual to be made responsible for maintaining contact after the closing with each affected household. This could be a union counselor, a professional outreach worker not working for a single agency, or a laid-off worker either working for pay or as a volunteer. This intervention should be as unobtrusive as possible, since considerations of privacy may in many cases outweigh the desirability of maintaining contact with the unemployed.

One way in which this contact may be maintained is for the individual to act as a catalyst for organizing worker recreational activities: softball teams, hot dog roasts, picnics, breakfast clubs, job clubs, and so on. The idea is to give the organizer a reason to stay in contact with families to assess their needs. Also, and equally important, the laid-off workers need to participate in group activities as one kind of coping behavior.

Employment services and referral. Because all nonretired workers are required to visit state employment services offices regularly in order to receive unemployment compensation, employment services' counselors should be mandated to make referrals for obvious problems not directly related to employment. Although employment services agencies are otherwise not well-equipped to perform a centralized access and referral role, their regular contact with workers is an advantage that should not be neglected.

Address files for the laid-off. Companies responsible for massive layoffs should be strongly urged, and probably required by law, to provide information needed by public agencies in order to contact affected workers and to do so as soon as plans for layoffs are final. Ideally, detailed information on every worker's employment experience and skills, interest in further training and education, medical and other personal and household characteristics should, *with the worker's informed consent,* be placed in a computer file where it can be analyzed to develop an individualized package of diagnostic services and other assistance appropriate to the needs of that worker and his or her dependents. Such information can be most readily assembled prior to termination, with the cooperation of both management and unions. The resulting personal data file must be safeguarded to prevent abuse; however, its existence is, on balance, a benefit to workers since it so greatly facilitates all subsequent efforts by service agencies, supports an adequate system of monitoring and accountability, and, finally, permits research to evaluate human services responses to the crisis. Because of concern over privacy, there may be great resistance to the sharing of information about workers with formal agencies. Some unions, for example, have by-law provisions forbidding the release of personal information on members. This concern for privacy has not proven to be as big an obstacle to action outside the United States. In Sweden, for example, *all* laid-off workers are continually accounted for by a highly sophisticated, nationwide computer system (see Harrison & Bluestone, 1982). Evaluations of this system have suggested that it is very efficient and effective, although perhaps expensive.

Importance of social networks. Existing, naturally occurring networks of association—friendship, kinship—should be used for information and referral whenever possible. Recent research has confirmed the importance, in neighborhoods and communities, of an informal network of self-help practices (Silverman, 1980; Froland et al., 1981; Warren, 1981; Rayman, 1982). This network operates in the shadow of the formal system to provide support for individuals and families in time of need. For instance, for several months following the Youngstown closing, a group of terminated workers met regularly for breakfast. Further research is needed to evaluate various methods by which the formal services system can support and use, but not supplant, these informal helping networks.

Income-Related Services

Continuing income maintenance programs are an important component of any intervention strategy aimed at reducing stress. Beyond the fairly standard compensation payments provided to workers in most plant closings, there are unfulfilled needs for special kinds of financial help. For instance, most terminated workers will soon lose their group health insurance coverage. The community must act quickly if workers are to be provided with relatively inexpensive alternate group coverage. At a later time, continuing loss of income may cause workers to miss home mortgage payments. If these homeowners' investments are to be protected, alternate payment terms must be worked out in cooperation with community leaders. In smaller communities, a substantial permanent layoff of workers can threaten property values and business incomes on a large scale throughout the community. In these instances, continuing income maintenance programs may be essential to the stability and viability of those places. Similarly, special state or federal aid may be needed to fill the revenue gap created in the public sector, so that essential services are maintained and government can function effectively as the community's agent for eventual revitalization.

Beyond these financial aids, consideration should be given to how best those special mental health and other human services required by affected workers and their families could be supported. Since this should not be done at the expense of others eligible for and in need of such services, the best mechanism may be a deferred payment plan or emergency revolving loan pool. This would allow workers to pay for present services while minimizing any stigma associated with financial dependency.

Financial counseling. In addition to income maintenance programs that supplement reduced incomes or delay payments for personal expenses, mental health agencies can assist workers in managing their financial affairs within reduced incomes. To accomplish this, a community mental health agency could subcontract, as in Youngstown, with a consumer credit counseling agency to deliver financial counseling to laid-off workers.

Another way in which these services might be delivered is for private lending institutions, brokerage firms, or even lay firms that typically provide counseling for a fee to offer a small amount of counseling to the unemployed at no charge. One laid-off worker told us, "We've deposited our money in these institutions for years and they have made a great deal of profit. It's time they gave a small amount of it back now that we need it."

Employment Services

The primary focus of any communitywide response to a plant shutdown should be the creation of jobs to replace those that were lost. The community mental health system should supplement this focus on jobs wherever possible. If the loss of a job is the major stimulus of mental and emotional problems, then the replacement of that job will go a long way toward solving those problems.

Mental health professionals may participate in the employment or reemployment process in many ways. Some of these are as follows.

Employment services and mental health. Every state distributes unemployment compensation, offers some training or retraining programs, and helps workers look for jobs through a system of local bureaus of employment services. As a result, employment counselors come into contact with many, but not all, workers who have been laid off. Mental health professionals should develop working relationships with these counselors to facilitate outreach to workers. Even more important, mental health professionals should thoroughly familiarize themselves with all of the programs and procedures of the employment bureaus, so that they can make appropriate referrals from the mental health to employment services system. It would be appropriate to establish a similar relationship with private sector employment agencies as well.

Job clubs and job fairs. Some communities, notably in Indiana and Michigan, are promoting job clubs and job fairs through the community mental health system in cooperation with the employment services system. Laid-off workers in job clubs periodically meet to discuss job possibilities and offer each other support (see Northeast-Midwest Institute, 1982). Job fairs allow prospective employers to meet with workers in much the same way as corporate recruiters meet with college student prospects. Mental health agencies may lend staff workers, provide facilities, and offer other support as required.

It is not yet known to what extent workers are able to obtain jobs in this fashion. It is also not yet known how cost effective these programs might be. What appears to be the case, however, is that workers are kept active in pursuing alternatives to unemployment and its accompanying isolation and depression. For this reason alone, these programs should continue to be thoroughly explored.

Retraining and education. Retraining and education programs (e.g., the TRA program of the U.S. Department of Labor, CETA, and others) have been widely critized because they are extremely expensive and, for the most part, do not boast even moderate rates of success in securing jobs for the unemployed.

Despite their problems, proposals to cut back these programs raise several questions regarding the potential mental health impacts of such cuts. If active participation following job loss is an important coping behavior, especially for workers not quickly reemployed, then these employment-related programs may be serving a valuable mental health need for workers. No research of which we are aware explores this possibility directly, but it should be a major item on the agenda for future research.

Even though publicly subsidized programs may be cut back, other possibilities exist. At present, laid-off workers who seek retraining or education cannot deduct tuition expenses from their federal taxes. One possibility is that workers who have been laid off for a substantial time be permitted by law to deduct the investment in their own skills and improved value to employers (Vaughan, 1981).

Another possibility is to offer qualified workers or members of their families scholarships to college and universities. At Youngstown State University, several hundred children of laid-off steelworkers were given four-year scholarships to complete their education. This may have served to relieve some of the financial and emotional stress on affected households.

Mental and Physical Health

Costs for health care have dramatically escalated in the last twenty to thirty years. This is, in part, the result of new treatments and a plethora of diagnostic tests produced by advances in medical science. Consequently, the public is increasingly unable to afford what is considered to be normal and necessary medical treatment without insurance or public subsidy. Loss of a job means for most workers that their ability to pay for health care is greatly reduced. Companies typically terminate health insurance soon after workers are let go, leaving the unemployed the choice of assuming the relatively high cost of insurance and/or treatment themselves or risking medical and financial catastrophe. Few public programs exist to alleviate this problem. Consequently, the loss of health care benefits may in and of itself produce mental and emotional problems for laid-off workers and their families.

As observed in Chapter 4 and in other studies of unemployment, mental and emotional problems arising out of stress and depression may manifest themselves as psychomatic illnesses (e.g., headaches, backaches, weakness, and so on). One result is that the unemployed person's perceived need for treatment of physical health problems may be increased; but this need cannot be paid for. A second result is that workers with physical health problems may be less desirable to potential employers or have less energy for job search.

From a public policy standpoint, then, it is important that laid-off workers have access to health care services and receive appropriate health care when required. Some of the ways in which this might be accomplished are discussed below.

What corporations might do. Corporations that are shutting down facilities may help to alleviate potential physical health/ mental health problems. Where resources permit, corporations should extend as far as possible into the future health care benefits for those who are laid off. These benefits need not cover ancillary services like dentist or oculist services but should be oriented instead toward major medical needs.

Corporations that have their own in-house health care facilities (e.g., company physicians, nurses, and the like) may, as part of their out-placement program for workers, use company facilities to offer physicals or health care for minor ailments. This might help to identify workers who have serious health or mental health problems requiring further treatment or who are at risk of such problems.

Finally, corporations—either those that are shutting down or those with philanthropic interests—might consider programs addressing the health care needs of laid-off workers. The substance and structure of such programs are discussed below.

What community mental health professionals can do. Community mental health professionals should play an active role in health care issues. A major motive for this is not only that workers will be helped in some way, but also that the ability of mental health workers to identify workers with mental and emotional problems will be enhanced. If some workers are experiencing physical health problems induced by stress or depression, then they may seek help from physicians who are prepared to treat illness primarily in terms of its physical symptoms. Consequently, workers with mental problems may never be treated in the mental health system.

Two programs illustrate ways to combat this problem. First, mental health professionals may offer workshops or seminars for physicians, especially those in family practice, on the possibility of their receiving patients with psychosomatic illness related to employment status. These programs are inexpensive to deliver and appear worth the effort. Second, mental health professionals may act as an impetus for establishment of a health care referral network, through which patients entering the physical health care systems are evaluated and diagnosed and then referred to appropriate mental health service delivery systems. A major feature of this system would be the tracking of referred patients to ensure that they made the transition from one system to the other.

What the community can do. A communitywide response may be required to deal with the health care problem. A program of the Detroit-Downriver Community Conference Economic Readjustment Program illustrates one way in which human services can be inexpensively delivered to those who need them. In 1981, a group of local public officials, health and human services providers, health insurance agencies (Blue Cross and Blue Shield), labor union leaders, and local merchants and industrialists formed a health care referral network. A staff of trained health care professionals was established in a highly visible, central location. Unemployed workers with health problems were screened there, and those with health problems were referred to one of several hospitals or clinics where physicians and other health care professionals donated their time and facilities to provide free or inexpensive services to workers, including physical examinations.

Unemployed workers with health problems may not be hired by firms conducting their own preemployment physicals. To avoid this problem, the program provides laid-off workers with free preemployment physicals in order to discover and treat problems before workers are sent to job interviews.

Getting Laid-off Workers Out of Isolation

Some laid-off workers may become increasingly isolated from the social activity and interpersonal relationships they enjoyed while being employed. Isolation may occur for a variety of reasons. Workers may blame themselves for the loss of a job and may seek to avoid contact with others. Some may feel embarrassed, inadequate, or remorseful, making social interaction difficult. Most likely, workers, whose interpersonal relationships were sustained by common experiences in the work place, will drift apart as individuals move away, take up new interests, or find replacement jobs.

Isolation is dysfunctional not only for the worker, but also for the mental health system. In the case of the workers, isolation may tend to precipitate or exacerbate mental and emotional problems brought on or made worse by job loss. Participation in activities involving others may be an effective antidote or therapeutic tool (e.g., Fineman, 1979). Workers in isolation are problematic for mental health service providers. When workers withdraw, they become increasingly more difficult to identify, locate, and serve. It is, therefore, in the interest of workers and service providers to maintain involvement in social life.

The mental health community can stimulate worker participation and involvement in a variety of ways. Some of these, identified below, can be accomplished directly by the mental health system. Others might require the cooperation of service providers. Certainly all might be encouraged or supported by the mental health community.

Programs or activities that foster participation, but which also may lead some workers to secure jobs, should be developed. Examples of these include the following.

Job Clubs. As observed above, job clubs are informal groups of workers who meet regularly to share information on possible job openings or opportunities in the community. These clubs have been very effective not only in helping workers find jobs, but also in bringing to light worker problems that might be solved by the group. Mental health staffers might assist these groups by periodically attending meetings, supplying job information, providing meeting facilities, and so on.

Retraining and education. The effectiveness of retraining or education programs in assisting workers in obtaining jobs is highly controversial (Buss et al., 1983). Regardless of the effectiveness of these programs for employment, they may be important for the psychological well-being of workers. Workers in retraining or education programs are forced to regularly attend classes, complete work toward a goal. These may be important factors when the alternative may be for a worker to sit at home and brood about his personal situation. Programs of this type may be difficult to encourage, since in many cases workers might be forced to pay for them out of their own pockets.

Mental health service providers can be helpful in these programs as a referral source for potential students with whom they come in contact. They might offer mental health facilities as program sites. They might also wish to actively support or encourage the development of these programs.

Laid-off workers as staff members. No one knows the status of laid-off workers in the community better than the workers themselves. In order to test this hypothesis, we asked workers in our study to list the names of as many coworkers as possible. Beside each name we asked them to indicate the current employment status of the worker and other information about how the worker was coping with job loss. Some workers only listed a dozen names. Others, however, were able to list nearly a hundred names with accompanying detailed information.

The mental health community could greatly benefit by including some laid-off workers on their staffs to act as liaison agents between service providers and potential clients. Programs in Northern Wales of which we are aware have been highly successful in this regard.

Recreation and mental health. Recreational activities such as block parties, field trips, sporting events, picnics, and so on, are excellent ways to stimulate participation by unemployed workers. These activities provide the vehicle or the excuse to draw workers out of self-imposed isolation. They may also assist workers in indirect ways as well: A worker may come to a block party and hear about a job opening from a neighbor.

Political Involvement. Laid-off workers may become embittered by termination of their jobs. Some may blow off steam by discussing the situation with friends, arguing at local taverns, expressing feelings to counselors, or speaking at union halls. Most, however, will not speak out and many will internalize their frustration with dysfunctional effect. We believe that, within reason, workers can become actively involved in job rallies, public meetings, letter writing campaigns, and other political activities as a way of venting frustration and anger at the loss of a job. Other activities involving violence or illegality are not to be suggested or condoned.

It is not appropriate for public sector mental health service providers to develop these activities. However, individual workers as clients might be encouraged to become more involved in the politics of employment.

Self-help and social networks. We have observed that self-help groups and social networks, many of which encompass things already mentioned, are important mechanisms in helping workers to cope with job loss and to locate new jobs. The ways in which mental health service providers can create, assist, maintain, or enhance these groups or networks are virtually uncountable. As an important service delivery strategy component, mental health workers should seek innovative ways of working with these groups.

Perhaps one caveat should be mentioned regarding participation and mental health. Mental health participation or presence in these activities should be as unobtrusive as possible. It is not the role of the mental health service provider to impose the formal helping system on the natural, informal relationships among workers and others in the community. Instead, it is to use the vast resources available in the formal helping system to enrich the informal relationships. Programs of this sort wil probably not work if the institutional character of the system becomes highly visible.

Preparation of Mental Health Staff

In-service training. Mass unemployment may present mental health staff workers with situations they have not frequently encountered. The typical client of a mental health or other human service agency is not the same as that produced by a plant closing. A vast majority of these laid-off workers will never have used mental health services in the past, and probably would not have required them. It is also likely, given their income and health insurance benefits, that any past contacts would have been with other than public mental health service agencies; for example, employee benefits often allow workers to visit private alcoholic clinics for problems with drinking.

Mental health professionals must booome sensitized to the special needs of the unemployed, especially when these differ from the usual problems presented for service. In-service training thus should be offered to staff workers. As part of this training, staff workers should be encouraged to share their successes and failures in helping the unemployed.

Victims-by-proxy. Professionals in health and mental health are likely to experience emotional problems themselves in the course of dealing with clients. These problems may develop into staff burnout. Staff emotional problems may occur because staff workers empathize too deeply with clients, feel frustrated at their inability to help many of those in need, fear that their efforts will leave some clients worse off, or are overwhelmed by a crushing caseload.

Winget and Umbenhauer (1982) pointed out, in their study of the effects of disasters on mental health professionals delivering services to victims of these crises, that the mental and emotional problems of victims might be transferred to those offering help. Professionals may become victims-by-proxy. This phenomenon may also affect staff workers delivering services to the unemployed.

It is important for mental health planners and administrators to include, as an adjunct to their service delivery, programs intended to ameliorate the potential mental and emotional problems of staff workers. Ironically, some of these programs may resemble those offered to the unemployed. Other possible programs are reviewed by Winget and Umbenhauer (1982).

The Role of State and Federal Governments

It is unlikely that in the near future state and federal governments will be able to play a major role in delivering or financing mental health and other human services to those communities affected by mass unemployment. There are at least two reasons for this: (1) the large number of plant closings and communities in need probably lies considerably outside the capacity of states or the federal government to satisfy demand; and (2) with relatively scarce resources, efforts to assist communities will probably be largely devoted to economic development and revitalization activities. But, in spite of their limited role, state[3] and federal[4] governments can do many constructive things.

Funding for demonstration projects. Many community mental health agencies lack the capacity to develop innovative progams or services for the unemployed. This is partly because they typically are forced to choose between maintaining their traditional services at previous levels or diverting funds from normal services into new and untried programs.

State and federal agencies can provide guidance and limited funds to encourage innovative efforts by local service providers. Given what we know of the mental health needs of the unemployed, funding for these projects should not be used merely to supplement traditional forms of service delivery.

Research on plant closings. In spite of the nation's experience with plant closings, very little collective knowledge has accumulated concerning the best, most feasible ways to deal with them as a matter of public policy. This is certainly the case in the health and mental health fields.

It is important for the state and federal governments to increase the number of funded scientific studies of plant closings nationwide. This should include the funding of single case studies, as well as comparative studies where possible. State and federal governments also should ensure that existing publication clearinghouse organizations seek out plant closing reports, summarize or synthesize material in them, and disseminate them to communities in need and scholars in the field. This research need is discussed further in the final chapter.

State technical assistance teams. No one organization or individual in a community is responsible for anticipating plant closings, attempting to lessen their effects, and promoting a healthy social and economic recovery. As a result, communities are typically caught by surprise when a plant shuts down. One consequence of this is that efforts to deal with the crisis are often in disarray for an extended period of time. Needless to say, this may worsen matters in a community.

State mental health and human service agencies would be the most logical agencies to establish technical assistance teams and send them into affected communities on short notice. There they can help local agencies and individuals develop a response to a plant closing with a minimum of time and confusion. Knowledge and experience gained by these teams could be shared across the state and with federal agencies, so that successful policies and programs could be developed. Such an activity might also raise the awareness of and promote preparedness in other communities not yet affected by job losses but at risk.

CONCLUSION

The circumstances of communities in economic crisis do not make it easy to construct an effective mental health response. The probable lack of federal and state assistance, the uniqueness of each situation and community, the limited resources and knowledge base from which to build a response, and the ambiguous long-term nature of the battle that must be fought all make this a major challenge. Therefore, communities must depend primarily on themselves to make appropriate decisions and create needed new capacity, must plan carefully for the use of scarce resources, must be innovative, and must be persistent. The state and federal governments could be supportive of such communities to the extent that they would provide timely information on what other communities have done and encourage or require the participation of companies and unions in joint planning for the closing and its aftermath. Companies, unions, and associations of human services professionals also could help by identifying past successful community efforts to meet such crises and offering their technical assistance in replicating these successes. Community mental health agencies will not be the primary sources of services for unemployed workers, but they can be the catalyst for effective action.

Notes

1. The issues relating to costs and benefits are reviewed by Sclar (1982).
2. Researchers describing responses to a Michigan plant closing reported successful implementation of an in-plant counseling program developed with the cooperation of company, union, and United Way community services (Taber, Walsh, & Cooke, 1979). There, management representatives counseled salaried employees. UAW local officials were released full time by the company to counsel wage employees. The United Way provided these counselors with three days of training. "The purpose of the

in-plant counseling program was not to provide professional psychological guidance to employees. Instead, the counselors served primarily to diagnose problems, get their clients in contact with the appropriate agency, and follow up to ensure the client had in fact taken corrective actions." A manual designed to aid communities in developing prelayoff programs has been developed by Judson Stone and Charles Kieffer (1981) of the Six Area Coalition Community Mental Health Center, near Detroit.

3. One example of state involvement is provided in the *Planning Guidebook for Communities Facing a Plant Closure or Mass Layoff* (Office of Planning and Policy Development, State of California, 1982).

4. A book, *Responding to Economic Crisis: A Guidebook for Community Leaders and Human Service Professionals,* is currently being prepared by the authors for the Center for Work and Mental Health, National Institute of Mental Health.

Chapter 8

JOB LOSS AND THE
COMMUNITY MENTAL
HEALTH MOVEMENT

Developing an effective mental health response to job loss is part of a larger task: developing effective community programs to prevent environment-caused emotional disorders and to promote positive mental health.[1] This final chapter places the effort to deal with consequences of mass unemployment in the context of the broader community mental health movement and its original core beliefs.

First, the legislative and administrative history of community mental health is briefly described. Second, the beliefs and the limited theoretical base supporting the movement are outlined. Third, the critics' views of the movement's conceptual weaknesses and failures of execution are presented. Fourth, the extent to which analysis of the Youngstown research offers support for both the movement and its critics is discussed. This chapter ends with a discussion of future priorities for community mental health programs and research.

LEGISLATIVE AND ADMINISTRATIVE HISTORY

The proposal for a "national mental health program to assist in the inauguration of a wholly new emphasis and approach to care for the mentally ill" was made by President Kennedy in February 1963. Congress passed an amended version of the Community Mental Health Center Act in October of that year (President's Commission, 1978).

President Kennedy's proposal differed in major respects from all previous proposals for a federal mental health role. Rhetorically, it "emphasized primary prevention and treatment in community mental health centers" and moved "the primary focus of treatment for the mentally ill away from the state hospitals" (President's Commission, 1978, p. 316). Actually, the act itself did little to specify the nature of the program; in this respect, it followed the prevailing pattern of federal social legislation in this period (Lowi, 1969).

NIMH regulations, established in 1964, began to spell out the community mental health centers (CMHC) concept. The regulations stated that construction grant applicants "must present a plan for a coordinated program of at least five essential mental health services: in-patient services, emergency services, partial hospitalization (such as day care), out-patient services, and consultation and education services." Other services were recommended but not required.

In 1965, Congress amended the act to provide funds for staffing and operating the new centers. In 1970, the federal share of support was expanded, and all centers became eligible for funding for a maximum of eight years.

Not until 1975 did Congress attempt to define more precisely what is meant by community mental health. The 1975 act specified twelve "essential services," adding to the mandate

specialized services for children and the elderly, assistance to courts and other public agencies in screening individuals being considered for admission to state mental hospitals, follow-up care for those discharged from state mental hospitals, half-way houses for those discharged from mental institutions, and programs for alcoholism and drug abuse.

The 1975 legislation also contains

requirements for the organization and operation of such centers; provision of services; coordination of services with other entities and the development of an integrated system of care; staffing; availability of services; responsiveness to the community served; governing bodies; quality assurance; and related matters [President's Commission, 1978, p. 317].

Thus, the original, vague concept has evolved into a specified model containing a uniform set of programs with delivery-management arrangements.

It is noteworthy that while the early mandate placed a joint emphasis on prevention *and* treatment, subsequent guidelines emphasized treatment *as* prevention. In the first instance, it would seem that prevention would be construed as a proactive orientation that assists essentially normal individuals in avoiding emotional problems. Later, the emphasis seems to shift. Prevention is taken to mean assisting people with mental problems from developing more serious emotional disturbance. This subtle but real distinction has not been understood by many people and has led to a muddled state of affairs.

In 1978, there were 590 operating community mental health centers serving 43 percent of the U.S. population. All but 12 percent of these were either affiliated with or based in general or mental hospitals.

According to the 1978 President's Commission Report,

the major trend in the diagnostic composition of the centers' clients has been the decreasing percent of those diagnoses with depressive disorders and schizophrenia, counter-balanced

by an increase of those classified as socially maladjusted, no
mental disorder, deferred diagnosis, or non-specific disorder
[p. 319].

In 1975, 22 percent of those admitted to the centers' care
received the latter, relatively milder diagnoses.

From the beginning of the CMHC movement, the emphasis
at the centers has been on serving people of low-to-moderate
incomes but not, specifically, the unemployed. Both the initial
federal operating grants and the increasing reliance of the
mature centers on third-party payments for services have supported this emphasis. In 1975, of 919,000 persons receiving
care, 54 percent reported weekly family income of less than
$100 (President's Commission, 1978, p. 320).

THE COMMUNITY MENTAL HEALTH
MOVEMENT DEFINED

Like other social reform experiments of the 1960s, the community mental health movement was an intellectual and politi
cal response to the unmet needs of a minority. It shared all of
the identifying characteristics of the period's new social programs: overly optimistic interpretations of limited and incom-
plete research findings about causal relations and the efficacy
of new treatments (Aaron, 1978), a concern for the poor and
with poverty as a cause of other problems, a vague legislative
mandate, loosely decentralized administration. Consequently,
conflicting ideas about what the intention is, how these intentions could be carried out, and how well the programs are working are present to this day (e.g., Kupers, 1981).

Despite the initial vagueness and resulting variety, it is possible to identify those beliefs that constitute the intellectual
core of the movement. Passage of the Federal Community
Mental Health Centers Act demonstrated and solidified the
rise to power of the mental health professionals. This degree of
success was possible because of a widespread faith in the

ability of mental health experts to effectively manipulate the social environment (Musto, 1977).

Among professionals, the adoption of the community mental health orientation reflected several beliefs: "The value of prevention and education, early detection, crisis intervention, and the strong possibility that perhaps two-thirds of the population were psychiatrically ill" presenting "not an impossible task, but a gigantic opportunity for social progress" (Musto, 1977). Still more specifically, the consensual core of the movement consisted of these tenets (Langsley, 1977):

(1)   commitment to serving an entire community, not just the person "who comes seeking help" or suffers an acute mental disorder;

(2)   a commitment to "continuity of care," "consideration of all etiological factors," and "use of all appropriate treatment methods"—an eclecticism that implies

(3)   "use of multidisciplinary teams" and "linkages with the human service network";

(4)   emphasis on prevention, although not to the exclusion of direct services to those needing them (Bolman, 1969);

(5)   avoidance of hospitalization where possible;

(6)   a focus on "health rather than illness"; and

(7)   citizen participation, education, and accountability.

Finally, a belief in poverty, racism, and powerlessness as contributors to mental illness and a concern for the poor and racial minorities have also characterized the movement.

The Movement Criticized

It is possible to criticize the movement in terms of its core beliefs and in terms of its ability to put these beliefs into practice. Both types of criticism are evident in recent writings that seek to evaluate the first one and one-half decades of experience of the community mental health centers program.

Among the critics are those who believe the movement erred in its departure from "a psychiatric base in medicine." These critics often are psychiatrists by profession. For instance, one psychiatrist argues that the preventive orientation emphasized by some centers is not supported by sufficient research and tested theory regarding how to design an effective program of prevention:

the further they (community mental health programs) deviate from a medical base, the more controversy results, with less success. . . . Looked at carefully, the ones that were not successful were, for the most part, those that attempted to attack broad social issues, such as racism, poverty, and education, as issues to be solved by the mental health center rather than concentrating their clinical efforts on treating the casualties of such systems [Ewalt, 1977].

On the other hand, there are those who criticize the *lack* of emphasis on prevention and "indirect services" in most local programs (Snow & Newton, 1976). The President's Commission on Mental Health in its 1978 report noted that "important questions have been raised about the centers program." They elaborated the division among critics as follows:

Community mental health centers recently have been subjected to heated criticism. Some observers point out the relatively limited role centers have played in key areas such as prevention. Others criticize them for straying from traditional psychiatric concepts and medically-oriented mental health care (President's Commission, 1978).

Critics and supporters of the community mental health program differ over its efficacy in meeting critical objectives. For instance, Chu and Trotter (1974) have claimed there is no evidence that the community mental health program reduces mental hospital admissions. On the other hand, Doidge and

Rodgers (1976) concluded, from a study conducted in Wyoming, that "(1) counties with comprehensive mental health services had a significantly lower admission rate than the state hospital . . . ; (2) when a county initiated or expanded its community mental health services, its admission rate decreased; and (3) admission rates increased in counties without mental health services."

Many of the movement's problems, and especially its problem in implementing the goal of prevention, can be traced to the lack of an adequate empirically based theory of intervention (Perlmutter, Vayda, & Woodburn, 1976). One defender of the movement noted in 1974 (MacDonald, Hedberg, & Campbell, 1974), "there are many professionals who are predicting the eventual demise of community mental health because of its failure to develop a relevant conceptual model for community intervention."

The lack of theory and subsequently the disappointment of many with program performance has led to more explicit conflicts over what the goals and limits of the movement should be, a fragmenting of the earlier appearance of consensus. One of the most severe critics of community mental health claims, "If one reviews the literature, it is apparent that no explicit, universally accepted set of goals has been provided for the mental health centers' programs. This in itself is a basic problem which will continue to plague the program and make effective evaluation impossible" (Gardner, 1977).

This critic also believes that the movement made the wrong response to studies demonstrating "the importance of the social environment and a variety of stresses in the onset and chronicity of the psychoses." The chosen response consisted of adopting "a public health model" over a "therapeutic approach" and attempting to construct interventions requiring "a broad range of competencies and coordination between many mental health, health, and social service disciplines." He concludes that: "both of these themes, the public health model and the coordination of an expanding number of disciplines in social interventions, were an invitation to interdisciplinary warfare and a power struggle from which the mental health field has yet to recover" (Gardner, 1977).

In summary, there is one line of criticism that argues against the adoption of a "preventive" or "public health" model and another that sees most centers as doing too little to develop such interventions. Similarly, there are those who believe the efforts toward interdisciplinary and eclectic staffing and treatment, and the compatible efforts to integrate mental health services with other community human services, are desirable but inadequately executed; there are others who see this direction as false and destructive.

PREVENTION:
BARRIERS AND RECOMMENDATIONS

Primary prevention means lowering the incidence of emotional disorder (1) by reducing stress, and (2) by promoting conditions that increase competence and coping skills. Primary prevention is concerned with populations not yet affected by individual breakdown, especially with groups at high risk. It is proactive—it often seeks to build adaptive strengths through education and reduce stress through social engineering [President's Commission, 1978].

The 1978 President's Commission on Mental Health Task Panel on Prevention identified five barriers to primary prevention[2] efforts: (1) a society that is oriented toward dealing with rather than preventing crises; (2) the threat that primary prevention poses to some people "because its very nature may raise sensitive issues of social and environmental change and/ or issues about one's right to be left alone"; (3) the history, traditions, and values of mental health professions built on strategies of repairing existing dysfunctions; (4) the fact that support mechanisms (such as third-party reimbursement, treat-

ment staff) are not geared toward prevention; (5) the pa
tation away from prevention, which requires that, befc ͜uch
programs can thrive, funds and staff must be wrested away
from other approaches, new administrative structures charged
with promoting the development of primary prevention must be
created, a supply of trained personnel must be generated, and
support must be found for research in primary prevention (President's Commission, 1978, pp. 1836-1837).

The Task Panel listed as possible high priorities for preventive program development:

> Programs with strong theoretical promise for success affecting
> potentially large numbers of people, e.g., . . . helping groups of
> people who experience sudden or extreme stresses such as
> infant death, *job loss,* or marital disruption.

> Programs aimed at improving broad social situations with potentially great impact on millions of people. . . . Examples include
> the potentially damaging mental health consequences of:
> (a) *unemployment,* discrimination, and *lack of job security*
> [President's Commission, 1978, p. 1838; emphasis added].

In contrast to this relatively optimistic view, the Commission's Research Task Panel suggested that much more research was needed before the merits of primary prevention programs could be established. It should also be noted that little attention has been paid in recent years to what Dooley and Catalano (1980) term "proactive primary prevention," that which attempts to remove potential risk factors from the environment. In the case of employment and mental health, such a strategy might aim at ensuring immediate reemployment of those who lose jobs or even at reducing the total national or local incidence of unemployment. However, most writing about primary prevention has focused on the need for "reactive primary" efforts to inoculate the populations at risk against the effects of environmental stressors by improving their adaptation and coping abilities (Dooley & Catalano, 1980).

A major employment crisis, such as occurred in Youngstown, may be considered an appropriate test of the current state of knowledge and practice in local community mental health centers and, therefore, the kind of further action and research required to fulfill the promise of effective prevention programs. An employment crisis, in other words, constitutes

(1)   a sudden increase in stresses originating in the social environment that were predicted to intensify or trigger mental health problems;

(2)   a crisis placing at risk a group widely scattered throughout an entire community and ultimately likely to affect every member of the community;

(3)   an opportunity to test the community mental health movement's core beliefs about the value of early detection, crisis intervention, education, and prevention; and

(4)   an opportunity to test the movement's commitment to employ eclectic treatment modes and work with other human services in developing the responses that are most appropriate to individual needs.

The prior program orientations of the two (Eastern and Western) community mental health centers serving the affected county helped to determine their responses to the crisis. Of the two, the Eastern Center, which received the emergency grant, possessed the stronger tradition of communitywide, street-level outreach. In its earliest days, all professional staff operated either entirely out of the community or in one of seven small inconspicuous satellite centers located in storefronts, church basements, and the like. Early staff hiring decisions emphasized street-level human relations skills rather than credentials. By the time the steel crisis occurred, this early orientation had greatly diminished. Although some of the early staff remained, they were no longer authorized to meet with clients outside the newly established center. Later hiring emphasized academic degrees and other formal credentials.

It is probable that the mental health center staff and its administrators were oriented to the day-to-day operation of the center. Thus, while the center began an outreach preventive movement to some extent, the pressure from its clientele led to a slow reorganization of the center to be more in line with a professional treatment (reactive) orientation with a fixed clientele.

Although one center was designated the emergency grant recipient, about one-half of the affected workers in the county lived in the catchment area served by the second center. The latter lacked a history of vigorous community outreach efforts. Its operations were confined to a newly completed building near a large Catholic hospital and away from major streets. The Western Center's acting director attended planning sessions dealing with the crisis; however, the center made no program changes or outreach efforts on behalf of the workers.

By the time the steel crisis emerged, each center had lost some of its initial flexibility of funds and programs. The centers were more concerned with maintaining their various client bases and, evidence suggests, viewed the unemployment problem as a short-term crisis with little potential for maintaining or further consolidating the financial basis of the centers.

How, then, does the previously described response of the community mental health system match up with the beliefs and theories advocated by the community mental health movement? The steel crisis response illustrates the difficulty of spontaneously developing effective programs of prevention and in reaching people with problems less severe than those generally classified as pathologies or breakdowns.

In-depth discussions with local mental health administrators produced a portrait of people who were frustrated and floundering. They appeared to have been surprised by the lack of response to their efforts to reach workers through media publicity, mass meetings, the union hall walk-in center, and other means. Nor were they able to identify the preexisting models for successful outreach to such groups or for treatment of services appropriate to recently terminated workers.

The results of the Youngstown investigation indicate why this was likely to be the case. What little academic research exists on plant closings and their social and psychological effects is silent on the design of outreach or human services programs of this sort (Dooley & Catalano, 1980). It is reasonable, therefore, to conclude that existing theory and practice are not sufficiently developed to allow for dissemination of information to community mental health agencies on how to respond to such crises.

The local mental health system did not act, with one exception, as a coordinator of other human services; no integrated services effort was made on behalf of the workers and others affected by the crisis. There was no authority granted to the community mental health center to coordinate other public or private service agencies. To the contrary, in Ohio, at both state and local levels, there are probably fewer integrating administrative and funding mechanisms in place than in most states in the nation. A contractual arrangement with the existing credit counselling service provided by a private family services agency constitutes the one significant effort by the community mental health center to formally link its services with those of other local agencies.

Because of the enormous conceptual and practical tasks required for any effort to integrate across functional responsibilities, it would be unfair to characterize the absence of an integrated response to the crisis as a failure of the community mental health centers. Certainly they lacked the formal authority or control over resources to overcome the normal barriers to services integration (Redburn, 1977).

The absence of coordination in the face of a diversity of individual and family situations calling for different combinations of effort by separate agencies reemphasizes the need for long-term efforts to build integrated delivery systems with strong information and referral, outreach, and diagnosis components. Such efforts can be successful only if they begin well before a crisis.

IMPLICATIONS FOR THE COMMUNITY MENTAL HEALTH MOVEMENT

From its beginnings, the community mental health movement has suffered from vagueness about whether indirect services, especially prevention, were to be a major responsibility. Operationally, as federal funding winds down, the task of developing and maintaining a primary prevention capability in local centers becomes even harder. Snow and Newton (1976) have written about the difficulty of maintaining such a commitment:

> The proposals regarding direct mental health services represented a kind of progressive, liberal reform. They were necessary to correct inequities and limitations in the system of service delivery and were relatively easy to accept. In contrast, the indirect service task implied a more radical change. By their nature, indirect services involved the greatest degree of change from a medical identity, in organizational structure and in ideology. They required the development of public health, consultation, and community intervention approaches which traditionally have been resisted by clinical psychology, psychiatry, and the other mental health disciplines. The indirect services task was consistently viewed with great ambivalence and . . . never was given clear definition or substantial support [1976, pp. 582-583].

On paper, prevention of mental illness among at-risk groups continues to be a "high priority objective" of the community mental health centers program (Jewell et al., 1980). Ironically, the prevention of mental illness was, as of 1980, "undefined on a program-wide basis." This conclusion is drawn in an internal "exploratory evaluation" of CMHC (Jewell et al., 1980). From an evaluator's standpoint, prevention also remains one of the most problematic of the program's components (p. 15). The exploratory evaluation finds that consultation and education (or C & E, which is the nearest programmatic equivalent of a preventive component) is among the "most troublesome service areas." The report's tone and conclusions are consistent with the recent pessimism about the effects of government social programs. It notes, "mental illness appears multifaceted in origin, and it appears that CMHC-initiated preventive measures can be expected to make at most a minor contribution to 'prevention' in this area." This pessimism also reflects the reality that the program's initial funding base is shifting, a circumstance felt most sharply by the staffs of the community centers around the country:

> If the centers survive, . . . they may not necessarily remain CMHC's as envisioned in the federal program. Several directors predicted the demise of C & E and other preventive programs when federal support dries up [Jewell et al., 1980].

However, for most centers, this problem lies in the future. The past and present lack of preventive programming must be explained otherwise. Among the greatest obstacles are the lack of adequate theory, the difficulty of reaching and organizing at-risk groups, and the necessity, difficulty, and cost of tailoring programming to the particular crisis at hand (Vayda & Perlmutter, 1977). If there is to be a community mental health program devoted in part to primary prevention, and if it is to achieve successes, such basic obstacles must be surmounted.

There is only a small body of practice and theory on which to draw. Indirect services, including prevention, accounted for less than five percent of staff time in 1972-1973 (Snow & Newton, 1976). The financing shift away from federal operating support and toward third-party reimbursement does nothing to encourage an increase in indirect services.

Action research to test and refine replicable intervention strategies must be pursued. The results should be packaged and disseminated. Above all, the potential contributions of non-mental health agencies to primary prevention should be acknowledged and coordination efforts included in the design of intervention strategies.

Such a development of the CMHC program's original promise of prevention will take time, especially as it works against the trend of shifting funding patterns and reduced ambitions. Those who believe in that original promise can take heart from this observation: Prevention has not failed; it has hardly been tried.

A RESEARCH AGENDA

Throughout the preceding discussion, a consistent theme has been the need to base mental health policy on adequate knowledge of the problem. The final obligation of the authors is to suggest some promising directions for inquiry concerning the effects of job loss and the appropriate public response.

Promising topics for research fall into three categories: (1) studies of the incidence and severity of mental health effects; (2) evaluations of formal efforts to reach and help affected workers and their families; and (3) other research on individual and group responses to job loss that supports the development of new public policy approaches. The most important research needs within each category are outlined below.

(1) *Incidence and severity of effects.* The evidence that job loss is stressful to many and harmful to some is, as previously noted, an insufficient basis for action. We not only need to be more precise in characterizing the aggregate level of emotional distress and disorder produced by mass umemployment, we need also to be able to say: (a) what circumstances surrounding job loss contribute to or diminish its harmful effects; (b) what personal characteristics or immediate environmental factors place some individuals at higher or lower risk of harm; and (c) by what processes and how rapidly the initial effects of job loss spread beyond those immediately affected.

To address variations in the circumstances of job loss, it will be necessary to study in systematic, comparative fashion a variety of such events. The Youngstown studies focus on an event of large absolute magnitude, but one occurring in a sizeable metropolitan area, so that the proportion of the work force directly affected is small. Other layoffs or closings may affect fewer workers but a larger percentage of a local labor force. It is important to examine how both the absolute scale and scale relative to the local economy influence the meaning and impacts of these events.

There are many other variations in the way job losses occur that can alter their expected effects. It obviously matters whether layoffs are temporary or permanent, are foreseen or occur without warning, are carefully planned and prepared for or not, occur in organized or unorganized shops, are accompanied by generous severance benefits or not, happen in a socially integrated and supportive community context or in an area of transiency and weak social and cultural institutions, and so on. Other significant variations concern the nature of the lost job and associated skills, particularly whether workers have acquired skills that are readily transferred to other firms or industries.

Focusing more directly on the affected workers, variations have been noted in the way job loss affects blue-collar versus white-collar workers, men versus women, minority versus nonminority workers, and so on. These demographic variations may be helpful in defining target groups for helping efforts, but more research is needed before it is possible to say more precisely what set of background characteristics puts individuals at greater risk of adverse effects. Ideally, this kind of research could produce a profile of the individual most likely to experience severe emotional problems and be used as a basis for concentrating most attention on people fitting this profile.

Studies of job loss impacts will also help with program design to the extent that they explain why some individuals cope much more successfully than others with unemployment. It is still unclear to what extent the measured impacts involve the generation of new emotional problems rather than the "uncovering" of preexisting disorders (Dooley & Catalano, 1980). A second area of insufficient information concerns the mechanisms or strategies that workers and families use to cope with job loss and related stress. It is unclear why an individual is predisposed toward one or another set of coping techniques and unclear, therefore, how readily workers and their families could be schooled to cope more effectively. Nor is it necessarily obvious how effective various coping methods are under varying personal circumstances. Coping behaviors should be studied across a wide range of individuals and situations in order to build basic understanding of the dynamic by which job loss leads either to profound damage or successful adaptation.

Another set of research needs concerns the spread of effects beyond those losing jobs to the larger community. The Youngstown studies suggest a pattern of slowly accumulating institutional deficits, financial losses, and deteriorating social relationships, perhaps over many months or years. By careful monitoring and analysis of social indicators, it should be possible to estimate the indirect, long-term, aggregate costs of job losses. Such information is needed not so much for the design of mental health or other social programs as for development of broader national and state policies concerning employment and regional development. The work of Harvey Brenner has already been widely used to indicate the approximate scale of aggregate effects and the promise of additional research that could extend and refine our understanding of where, how quickly, and by what processes the effects of job losses spread through communities and the larger society.

(2) *Evaluation of helping efforts.* The value of evaluation research is limited, as noted before, by the small number of programs directed at job loss. Major evaluation issues include (a) whether programs reach those most in need of external aid; (b) which service approaches are effective; and (c) what models for organizing service delivery result in effective programs.

Evaluation research is needed to establish how to reach a relatively small group of affected workers likely to experience major emotional problems. This targeting problem breaks down into subsidiary issues of whether a given strategy is properly timed, minimizes the bureaucratic burden on those seeking help, establishes an appropriate schedule and level of payment for services received, is not inordinately expensive, and does not put too much strain on local systems required to meet not only these needs but others. The issue of targeting should not, however, preclude judging the success of outreach efforts in other terms. Although most workers may not need much external aid, they may nevertheless improve their responses to job loss if given timely information, advice, and opportunities to participate in collective efforts to reduce the pain associated with a plant closing or similar events. Evidence presented in preceding chapters suggests that new approaches to reaching laid-off workers should be tried and evaluated, both in terms of targeting on those at greatest risk and of timely preventive aid to a broader group.

A second focus of evaluation research must be on the utility of particular services programs and other types of assistance. These other forms of aid include direct financial assistance and informal support from peers or others who do not have a formally assigned service responsibility. The evaluation issues are quite complex because the variety of programs and forms of assistance to be considered is great and the range of needs created by job loss is broad. The standards for judging the success of helping efforts include whether individuals are protected from pain or harm and also whether they learn more effective ways of dealing with such personal crisis. Evaluation must consider not only effectiveness but cost; therefore, the appropriate general question to be answered by such research is which combination of helping efforts is most cost effective. It is of particular interest whether the advantages of early intervention designed to prevent emotional problems from developing are necessarily offset by the cost of detecting a relatively small number of persons at risk and/or giving attention to many people who can cope just as effectively without it. This is a basic question facing those in the mental health field who believe in prevention.

The third focus of evaluation studies should be on models for organizing, administering, and financing efforts to help the unemployed. The experience of Youngstown indicates that many, if not most, service needs do not fall within the legal mandates or necessarily even the traditional functions of service providers. The innovative character of needed programs as well as the usual weakness of services coordination mechanisms require new forms of organization. One possibility is that state or federal government intervention will be useful, as in natural disasters, initially to pull together the plans and resources and quickly implement an appropriate helping response. The roles that community mental health agencies can play in organizing an effective services response to massive job loss should be a major focus of evaluation research.

(3) *Other research.* Basic research on how people respond, individually or collectively, to the shock of job loss will improve our understanding of its causal dynamics. This, in turn, will provide clues to what public policies are needed to minimize personal hardships and encourage more effective individual management of such potentially damaging events. It is striking how differently people interpret and react to similar situations. On the surface, it may appear that such differences are a function of differences of personality. However, research may show that how significant others initially respond to the laid-off person or interpret the event play a large role in determining responses. Research that focuses on the stages of response, the interaction of personality and social environment in shaping interpretation and behavior, and the process by which stresses spread outward from those initially affected to others will be valuable in guiding policy development and program design.

If this research agenda were pursued vigorously, it would build a sounder base of knowledge for mental health policies to deal with job loss. The resulting set of tested programs and their organization might constitute what we now lack: an effective strategy for meeting the mental health needs produced when large numbers of people are without work.

Notes

1. See Buss and Redburn (1982) and Buss and Redburn (1983b) for a review of these issues.
2. See Price et al. (1980) for a comprehensive review of prevention in community mental health.

References

Aaron, Henry. *Politics and the professors: The Great Society in perspective.* Washington, DC: Brookings Institution, 1978.

Aiken, Michael, Louis A. Ferman, & Harold L. Sheppard. *Economic failure, alienation and extremism.* Ann Arbor: University of Michigan, 1968.

Bagshaw, Michael, & Robert H. Schnorbus. The local-market response to a plant shutdown. *Economic Review: Federal Bank of Cleveland,* January 1980, 16-24.

Bakke, E. Wright. *Citizens without work.* New Haven, CT: Institute of Human Relations, Yale University Press, 1940.

Barling, P., & P. Handel. Incidence of utilization of public mental health facilities as a function of short-term economic decline. *American Journal of Community Psychology,* 1980, *8,* 31-40.

Barth, Michael C., & Fritzie Reisner. *Worker adjustment to plant shutdowns and mass layoffs.* Washington, DC: National Alliance of Business, August 1981.

Barton, Walter E., & Charlotte J. Sanborn (Eds.). *An assessment of the community mental health movement.* Lexington, MA: D. C. Heath, 1977.

Beck-Rex, M. Youngstown: Can this steel city forge a comeback? *Planning,* 1978, *44,* 12-15.

Bendick, Marc Jr., & Judith Radlinski Devine. *Workers dislocated by economic change: Is there need for federal employment and training assistance?* Washington, DC: Urban Institute, August, 1981.

Blau, Peter. *The dynamics of bureaucracy* (Rev. ed.). Chicago: University of Chicago Press, 1964.

Bolman, William. Toward realizing the prevention of mental illness. In Leopold Bellak and Harvey H. Barten (Eds.), *Progress in community mental health* (Vol. I). New York: Grune & Stratton, 1969.

Braginsky, D. D., & B. M. Braginsky. Surplus people: Their lost faith in self and system. *Psychology Today,* August 1975, *9,* 68-72.

Brenner, M. H. *Mental illness and the economy.* Cambridge, MA: Harvard University Press, 1973.

Brenner, M. H. Trends in alcohol consumption and associated illnesses: Some effects of economic changes. *American Journal of Public Health,* 1975, *65,* 1279-1292.

Brenner, M. H. *Estimating the social costs of economic policy: Implications for mental and physical health, and criminal aggression.* Report to the Congressional Research Service of the Library of Congress and Joint Economic Committee of Congress. Washington, DC: Government Printing Office, 1976.

Brenner, M. H. Personal stability and economic security. *Social Policy,* 1977, *8,* 2-5.

Buss, Terry F., & C. Richard Hofstetter. Communication, information, and participation during an emerging crisis. *Social Science Journal,* January 1981, *18,* 81-91.

Buss, Terry F., C. Richard Hofstetter, & F. Stevens Redburn. The psychology of mass unemployment: Some political and social implications. *Political Psychology,* (Fall/Winter 1980), *3,* 95-113.

Buss, Terry F., & F. Stevens Redburn. Evaluating human service delivery during a plant shutdown: A decision seminar application. *Journal of Health and Human Resources Administration,* 1980, *3,* 229-250.

Buss, Terry F., & F. Stevens Redburn. How to shut down a plant. *Industrial Management,* (1981) *33,* 4-10.

Buss, Terry F., & F. Stevens Redburn (Eds.). Health and human services responses to community crisis. *Journal of Health and Human Resources Administration,* 1981, Special Symposium Issue, 4.

Buss, Terry F., & F. Stevens Redburn. *Shutdown at Youngstown.* New York: SUNY Press, 1983. (a)

Buss, Terry F., & F. Stevens Redburn (Eds.). Administering mental health programs in a transitional economy. *Administration in Mental Health,* 1983, Special Symposium Issue, *10.* (b)

Buss, Terry F., F. Stevens Redburn, & Frank Costa (Eds.). Reemploying, retraining, and relocating displaced workers. *Journal of Health and Human Resources Administration,* 1983, Special Symposium Issue, 6.

Caplovitz, David. *Making ends meet: How families cope with inflation and recession.* Beverly Hills, CA: Sage , 1979.

Cassimatis, Emanuel. Mental health viewed as an ideal. *Journal of Psychiatry,* August 1979, *42,* 241-254.

Catalano, Ralph, & David Dooley. Economic predictors of depressed mood and stressful life events in a metropolitan community. *Journal of Health and Social Behavior,* 1977, *18,* 292-307.

Catalano, Ralph, & David Dooley. Does economic change provoke or uncover behavioral disorder? A preliminary test. In L. Ferman and J. Gordus (Eds.), *Mental Health and the Economy.* Kalamazoo, MI: W. E. Upjohn Institute for Employment Research, 1979.

Caudill, Harry M. *Night comes to the Cumberlands, A biography of a depressed area.* Boston: Little, Brown, 1963.

Chu, F. D., & S. Trotter. *The madness establishment.* New York: Grossman, 1974.

Cobb, S. Social support as a moderator of life stress. *Psychosomatic Medicine,* 1976, *38,* 300-314.

Cobb, S., & S. V. Kasl. *Termination: The consequences of job loss* (Report No. 76-1261). Cincinnati, OH: National Institute for Occupational Safety and Health, Behavioral and Motivational Factors Research, June 1977.

Cohn, R. M. The effects of employment status change on self attitudes. *Social Psychology*, 1978, *41*, 81-93.

Commerce-Labor Adjustment Action Committee. *Sharpening government's response to plant closings*. Washington, DC: U.S. Department of Labor, November 1979.

Cook, T. E. Psychosocial barriers to rehabilitation in Appalachia. *Rehabilitation Counseling Bulletin*, December 1967, *11*, 98-105.

Cowen, Emory L. Help is where you find it: Four informal helping groups. *American Psychologist*, April 1982, *37*, 385-395.

Cross, D., A. Barclay, & G. Barger. Differential effects of ethnic membership, sex, and occupation on the California Psychological Inventory. *Journal of Personality Assessment*, 1978, *42*, 597-603.

Dean, Alfred, & Dan Lin. The stress-buffering role of social support. *Journal of Nervous and Mental Disease*, 1977, *165*, 403-417.

Dohrenwend, Barbara S., & Bruce P. Dohrenwend. *Stressful life events: Their nature and effects*. New York: John Wiley, 1974.

Doidge, John R. & Charles W. Rodgers. Is NIMH's dream coming true? *Community Mental Health Journal*, 1976, *12*, 339-403.

Dooley, David, & Ralph Catalano. Money and mental disorder: Toward behavioral cost accounting for primary prevention. *American Journal of Community Psychology*, 1977, *5*, 217-227.

Dooley, David, & Ralph Catalano. Economic life and disorder changes: Time-series analysis. *American Journal of Community Psychology*, 1979, *7*, 381-396.

Dooley, David, & Ralph Catalano. Economic change as a cause of behavioral disorder. *Psychological Bulletin*, 1980, *87*, 450-468.

Dow, Leslie M. Jr. High weeds in Detroit: The irregular economy among a network of Appalachian migrants. *Urban Anthropology*, Summer 1977, *6*, 111-128.

Durman, Eugene C. The role of self-help in service provision. *Journal of Applied Behavioral Science*, Summer 1976, *12*, 433-443.

Eisenberg, Philip, & P. F. Lazersfeld. The psychological effects of unemployment. *Psychological Bulletin*, June 1938, *35*, 358-389.

Elder, Glen, & Richard C. Rockwell. Economic depression and postwar opportunity in men's lives: A study of life patterns and health. In Roberta Simmons (Ed.), *Research in Community and Mental Health*, 1 (1979), 249-303.

Engel, G. L. & A. H. Schmale. Psychoanalytic theory of somatic disorder. *Journal of American Psychoanalytic Association*, 1967, *15*, 334-365.

Ewalt, Jack R. The birth of the community mental health movement. In W. E. Barton and C. J. Sanborn (Eds.), *An assessment of the community mental health movement*. Lexington, MA: D. C. Heath, 1977.

Eyer, Joseph. Does unemployment cause the death rate peak in each business cycle? *International Journal of Health Sciences*, 1977, *7*, 625-662.

Ferman, Louis A. Remarks delivered before the Committee on Labor and Human Resources on the role of the worker in the evolving economy of the eighties. Washington, DC, September 18, 1980. (photocopy)

Ferman, Louis A., & John Gardner. Economic deprivation, social mobility, and mental health. In L. A. Ferman and J. P. Gordus (Eds.), *Mental health and the economy*. Kalamazoo, MI: W. E. Upjohn Institute for Employment Research, 1979.

Ferman, Louis A., & Jeanne P. Gordus (Eds.), *Mental health and the economy.* Kalamazoo, MI: W. E. Upjohn Institute for Employment Research, 1979.

Field, L. W., R. T. Ewing, & D. M. Wayne. Observations on the relations of psychosocial factors to psychiatric illness among coalminers. *Journal of Social Psychiatry*, 1957, 3, 133-145.

Figueira-McDonough, Josephina. Mental health among unemployed Detroiters. *Social Service Review*, September 1978, 52, 383-399.

Fineman, Stephan. A psychosocial model of stress and its application to managerial unemployment. *Human Relations*, 1979, 32, 323-345.

Foltman, Felician F. *White and blue collars in a mill shutdown.* Ithaca, NY: Cornell University Press, 1968.

Freudenburg, William, Linda M. Bacigalupi, and Cheryl Landoll-Young. Mental health consequences of rapid community growth. *Journal of Health and Human Resources Administration,* 1982, 4, 334-352.

Froland, Charles et al. *Helping networks and human services.* Beverly Hills, CA: Sage, 1981.

Furstenberg, Frank. Work experience and family life. In James O'Toole (Ed.), *Work and the quality of life. Resource papers for work in America.* Cambridge: MIT Press, 1974.

Gardner, Elmer A. Community mental health center movement: Learning from failure. In W. E. Barton and C. J. Sanborn (Eds.), *An assessment of the community mental health movement.* Lexington, MA: D. C. Heath, 1977.

Gold, Raymond L. *Industrial and community responses to a plant closing in Anaconda, Montana.* Final report to the Center for Work and Mental Health, National Institute of Mental Health, Washington, DC, May 1981.

Gordus, Jeanne. Studying the physical and mental health effects of job displacement. Response to Major Layoffs and Plant Closings, 1979, Michigan Department of Mental Health.

Gore, Susan. The effects of social support in moderating the health consequences of unemployment. *Journal of Health and Social Behavior,* 1978, 19, 157-165.

Gynther, M. White norms, Black MMPIs—A prescription for discrimination. *Psychological Bulletin,* 1972, 78, 386-402.

Haber, W., L. A. Ferman, & J. R. Hudson. *The impact of technological change.* Kalamazoo, MI: W. E. Upjohn Institute for Employment Research, 1963.

Hansen, Gary B., Marion T. Bentley, & Richard A. Davidson. *Hardrock miners in a shutdown: A case study of the post-layoff experience of displaced lead-zinc-silver miners.* Logan, UT: Economic Research Center, Utah State University, 1980.

Harrison, Bennett, & Barry Bluestone. The incidence and regulation of plant shutdowns. In F. S. Redburn and T. F. Buss (Eds.), *Public policies for distressed communities.* Lexington, MA: Lexington Books, 1982.

Hirsch, B. Natural support systems and coping with major life changes. *American Journal of Community Psychology,* 1980, 8, 159-172.

Ignatius, David. Who killed the steel industry? *Washington Monthly,* March 1979.

Jacobson, D. Time and work. Unemployment among middle-class professionals. Unpublished manuscript, Brandeis University, 1977.

Jahoda, M., P. F. Lazarsfeld, & H. Zeisel. *Marienthal: The sociography of an unemployment community.* Chicago: Aldine-Atherton, 1971.

Jahoda, Marie. The impact of unemployment in the 1930's and the 197‑ the British Psychological Society, August 1979, 32, 309-314.

Jensen, Arthur R. Bias in mental testing. New York: Free Press, 1980.

Jewell, Michael, Larry Beyna, Edward Yates, & Elinor Walker. Exploratory tion of the community mental health center program. Washington, DC. Department of Health, Education and Welfare, Office of Planning and Evaluat. March 1980.

Kaplan, B. H., J. L. Cassell, & Susan Gore. Social support and health. Medical Care, 1977, 15, 47-58.

Kasl, S., & S. Cobb. Some mental health consequences of plant closings and job loss. In L. A. Ferman and J. P. Gordus (Eds.), Mental Health and the Economy. Kalamazoo, MI: W. E. Upjohn Institute for Employment Research, December 1979.

Kasl, S., S. Gore, & S. Cobb. The experience of losing a job: Reported change in health symptoms and illness behavior. Psychosomatic Medicine, March/April 1975, 37, 106-122.

Kennedy, John F. Message from the President of the United States Relative to Mental Illness and Mental Retardation. Eighty-eighth Congress, First Session, U.S. House of Representatives, Document 58. Washington, DC: Government Printing Office, 1963.

Kielholz, B. Masked depression. Bern: Hans Huber, 1973.

King, Craig. The social impacts of mass layoff. Ann Arbor: Center for Research on Social Organization, University of Michigan, January 1982. (mimeo)

Komarovsky, Mirra. The unemployed man and his family: The effect of unemployment upon the status of the man in 59 families. New York: Dryden Press, 1940.

Kornblum, William. Blue-collar community. Chicago: Chicago University Press, 1974.

Kornhauser, Arthur W. Mental health of the industrial worker. New York: John Wiley, 1965.

Kupers, Terry A. Public therapy: The practice of psychotherapy in the public mental health clinic. New York: Free Press, 1981.

Landesberg, Gerald et al. (Eds.). Evaluation in practice. Washington, DC: National Institute of Mental Health, 1979.

Langsley, Donald G. Community mental health: A review of the literature. In W. E. Barton & C. J. Sanborn (Eds.), An assessment of the community mental health movement. Lexington, MA: D. C. Heath, 1977.

LeMaster, E. E. Blue-collar aristocrats: Life styles at a working-class tavern. Madison: University of Wisconsin Press, 1975.

Levin, Hannah. Work, the staff of life. Paper presented at the Annual Convention of the American Psychological Association, Chicago, September 1975.

Levitt, E. E., & B. Lubin. Depression: Concepts, controversies and some new facts. New York: Springer, 1975.

Lieberman, Morton A., & Leonard D. Borman. Self-help and social research. Journal of Applied Behavioral Science, 1976, 12, 455-463.

Liebow, Elliot. Tally's corner. Boston: Little, Brown, 1967.

Liem, G. Ramsay, & Joan Huser Liem. Social support and stress: Some general issues and their application to the problem of unemployment. In L. A. Ferman and J. P.

Gordus (Eds.), *Mental Health and the Economy.* Kalamazoo, MI: W. E. Upjohn Institute for Employment Research, December 1979.

Lipsky, D. B. Interplant transfer and terminated workers: A case study. *Industrial and Labor Relations Review,* 1970, *23,* 191-206.

Lipsky, Michael. *Street-level bureaucracy.* New York: Russell Sage, 1980.

Lowi, Theodore. *The end of liberalism: Ideology, policy and the crisis of public authority.* New York: W. W. Norton, 1969.

MacDonald, K. R., A. G. Hedberg, & L. M. Campbell. A behavioral revolution in community mental health. *Community Mental Health Journal,* 1974, *10,* 228-235.

Manusco, James. Coping with job abolishment. *Journal of Occupational Medicine.* September 1977, 19.

Maurer, Harry. *Not working: An oral history of the unemployed.* New York: Holt, Rinehart & Winston, 1979.

Mick, Stephen S. Social and personal cost of plant shutdowns. *Industrial Relations,* 1975, 203-208.

Musto, David F. The community mental health center movement in historical perspective. In W. E. Barton & C. J. Sanborn (Eds.), *An assessment of the community mental health movement.* Lexington, MA: D. C. Heath, 1977.

Nathanson, Josef. *Early warning information systems for business retention.* Washington, DC: Urban Consortium Information Bulletin, 1980.

Northeast-Midwest Institute. *Shutdown: A guide for communities facing plant closings.* Washington, DC: Northeast-Midwest Institute, 1982.

Office of Planning and Policy Development. *Planning guidebook for communities facing a plant closure or mass layoff.* Sacramento: State of California, June 1982.

Pearlin, L. I., & C. W. Radabaugh. Economic strains and the coping functions of alcohol. *American Journal of Sociology,* 1976, *82,* 652-663.

Perlmutter, Felice D., A. Vayda, & W. Woodburn. An instrument for differentiating programs in prevention-primary, secondary, and tertiary. *American Journal of Orthopsychiatry,* July 1976, *46,* 533-541.

Polivka, Larry, Allen W. Imershein, John Wesley White, & Lawrence E. Stivers. Human services reorganization and its effects: A preliminary assessment of Florida's services integration "experiment." *Public Administration Review,* May-June 1977, *37,* 264-269.

Powell, Douglas H., & Patricia Joseph Driscoll. Middle-class professionals face unemployment. *Society,* 1973, *10,* 18-26.

President's Commission on Mental Health. *Task Force Panel Report.* Washington, DC: Government Printing Office, 1978.

Price, Richard H., Richard F. Ketterer, Barbara C. Bader, & John Monahan (Eds.), *Prevention in mental health.* Beverly Hills, CA: Sage, 1980.

Pursell, Donald E. et al. *Trade adjustment assistance: An analysis of impacted worker benefits on displaced workers in the electronics industry.* Memphis: Center for Manpower Studies, Memphis State University, 1975.

Rayman, Paula. The world of not working: An evaluation of urban social service response to unemployment. *Journal of Health and Human Resources Administration,* 1982, *4,* 319-333.

Redburn, F. Stevens. On "human services integration." *Public Administration Review,* May-June 1977, *37,* 264-269.

Redburn, F. Stevens, & Terry F. Buss (Eds.). *Public policies for distressed communities.* Lexington, MA: Lexington Books, 1982.

Root, Kenneth. *Perspectives for community and organizations on job closings and job dislocation.* Ames: Iowa University Press, 1979.

Rueth, Thomas, & Abraham Heller. Unemployment: A factor in mental health crisis. *American Journal of Social Psychiatry,* 1981, *3,* 49-51.

Sadava, S. W., R. Thistle, & R. Forsyth. Stress, escapism and patterns of alcohol and drug abuse. *Journal of Studies on Alcohol,* 1978, *39,* 725-736.

Samuelson, Robert J. Backwards on jobs. *National Journal,* February 7, 1981.

Schlozman, Kay Lehman, & Sidney Verba. *Injury to insult: Unemployment, class and political response.* Cambridge, MA: Harvard University Press, 1979.

Schultz, George P., & Arnold R. Weber. *Strategies for displaced workers.* New York: Harper & Rowe, 1966.

Sclar, Elliot D. Social cost minimization: A national policy approach to the problems of distressed economic regions. In F. S. Redburn & T. F. Buss (Eds.), *Public policies for distressed communities.* Lexington, MA: Lexington Books, 1982.

Segall, A. The sick role concept: Understanding illness behavior. *Journal of Health and Social Behavior,* 1976, *17,* 163-170.

Seligman, M. E. Depression and learned helplessness and research. In R. J. Friedman and M. M. Katz (Eds.), *The psychology of depression: Contemporary theory and research,* New York: John Wiley, 1974.

Sheppard, Harold L. Worker reactions to job displacement. *Monthly Labor Review,* February 1965.

Sheppard, Michael et al. *Psychiatric illness in general practice.* London: Oxford University Press, 1966.

Silverman, Phyllis R. *Mutual help groups.* Beverly Hills, CA: Sage, 1980.

Slote, Alfred. *Termination: The closing at Baker plant.* New York: Bobbs-Merrill, 1969.

Snow, David L., & Peter M. Newton. Task, social structure, and social process in the community mental health movement. *American Psychologist,* August 1976, *31,* 582-594.

Squires, Gregory D. *Shutdown: Economic dislocation and equal opportunity.* Chicago: Illinois Advisory Committee to the U.S. Civil Rights Commission, 1981.

Steinberg, Laurence D., Ralph Catalano, & David Dooley. Economic antecedents of child abuse and neglect. *Child Development,* 1981, *52,* 975-985.

Stern, J. Consequences of plant closure. *Journal of Human Resources,* January 1973, *7,* 3-25.

Stone, Judson, & Charles Kieffer. *Pre-layoff intervention: A response to unemployment.* Detroit: Six-Area Coalition, Community Mental Health Center, 1981. (photocopy)

Strange, William. *Job loss: A psychosocial study of worker reactions to a plant closing.* Washington, DC: Employment and Training Administration, August 1977.

Taber, Thomas D., Jeffrey T. Walsh, & Robert A. Cooke. Developing a community-based program for reducing the impact of a plant closing. *Journal of Applied Behavioral Science,* 1979, *15,* 133-155.

Taylor, Verta, Alexander Ross, & E. L. Quarantelli. *Delivery of mental health services in disasters: The Xenia tornado and some implications.* Columbus: Disaster Research Center, Ohio State University, 1976.

Terkel, Studs. *Working.* New York: Random House, 1974.

Tessler, Richard, David Mechanic, & Margret Dimond. The effect of psychological distress on physician utilization. *Journal of Health and Social Behavior,* 1976, *17,* 353-364.

Vaughan, Roger J. Employment and training: What's wrong with the present system and what can be done about it? Washington, DC: Council of State Planning Agencies, July 1981.

Vayda, Andrea M., & Felice D. Perlmutter. Primary prevention in community mental health centers: A survey of current activity. *Community Mental Health Journal,* 1977, *13,* 343-351.

Waldron, J., G. Kerchauf, & C. Sutton. *Manual for the audio presentation of the personality research Form E.* Port Huron, MI: Research Psychologists Press, 1981.

Warheit, George J., Charles E. Holzer, Lynn Roberts & Joanne M. Buhl. *Integrated needs assessment approaches.* Florida State University, 1979. (mimeo)

Warren, Donald I. *Helping networks.* Notre Dame, IN: University of Notre Dame Press, 1981.

Warren, Rochelle. Stress, primary support systems, and the blue-collar woman. *Response to major layoffs and plant closings.* Lansing: Michigan Department of Mental Health, 1980.

Weeks, Edward C., & Sandra Drengacz. The non-economic impacts of community economic shock. *Journal of Health and Human Resources Administration,* 1982, *4,* 303-318.

Wilcock, R. C., & W. H. Franke. *Unwanted workers: Permanent layoffs and long-term unemployment.* New York: Free Press, 1963.

Wildavsky, Aaron. *Speaking truth to power.* Boston: Little, Brown, 1979.

Williams, L. K., F. F. Foltman, & N. A. Rosen. *Some social psychological correlates of a depressed area.* Ithaca, NY: New York State School of Industrial and Labor Relations, Cornell University Reprint 139, n.d.

Winget, Carolyn N. & Sandra L. Umbenhauer. Disaster planning: The mental health worker as victim-by-proxy. *Journal of Health and Human Resources Administration,* 1982, *4,* 363-373.

Zawadski, Bohan, & Paul Lazarsfeld. The psychological consequences of unemployment. *Journal of Social Psychology,* Jan. 1935, *6,* 224-251.

About the Authors

Terry F. Buss is Director of the Center for Urban Studies at Youngstown State University. He received his doctorate in political science from Ohio State University in 1976. He is the author of numerous articles in a variety of social science fields. His most recent book is *Shutdown at Youngstown: Public Policy for Mass Unemployment* (1983) coauthored with Steve Redburn. He is presently at work on two separate books examining the long-term effects of plant closings and the economic revitalization process in distressed communities.

F. Stevens Redburn is a Social Science Analyst in the Office of Policy Development and Research, the U.S. Department of Housing and Urban Development in Washington, D.C. He earned his doctorate in political science from the University of North Carolina. His research has been published in a variety of public policy and social science journals. Recently, along with Terry Buss, he has edited journal symposia for publications such as *Administration in Mental Health, Journal of Health and Human Resources Administration, Policy Studies Journal,* and *Policy Studies Review.* His research interests for future endeavors concern new modes of citizen participation in the public policy process.

Joseph Waldron is an Assistant Professor of Criminal Justice at Youngstown State University. He holds a doctorate from Ohio State University in developmental and forensic psychology. He has published many articles and conducted a number of funded research projects on computerized diagnostic evaluations. His most recent book, co-authored with Carol Sutton and Terry Buss, is entitled *Personal Computers in Criminal Justice* (1983).